Rescued by the LIGHT

A True Story

Andrea Edwards

 FriesenPress

Suite 300 - 990 Fort St
Victoria, BC, V8V 3K2
Canada

www.friesenpress.com

Copyright © 2016 by Andrea Edwards
First Edition — 2016

andreaedwards2016@hotmail.com
www.rescuedbythelight.com

All rights reserved.

No part of this publication may be reproduced in any form, or by any means, electronic or mechanical, including photocopying, recording, or any information browsing, storage, or retrieval system, without permission in writing from FriesenPress.

ISBN
978-1-4602-8617-3 (Hardcover)
978-1-4602-8618-0 (Paperback)
978-1-4602-8619-7 (eBook)

1. RELIGION, DEVOTIONAL

Distributed to the trade by The Ingram Book Company

Endorsement's for "Rescued by the Light"

"From Chile, South America, to chilly Alberta, Canada, Andrea Edwards' journey powerfully depicts God's supernatural intervention in the life of a hurting young girl longing to be loved. I was drawn into her story from the very first page. Thoughtful and engaging, Andrea skilfully paints the canvas of her life, including some very dark colours, and she is a trophy of God's grace, giving hope to others who find themselves in deep pain and despair."

Rev. Ron Mainse, *100 Huntley Street*

Andrea Edwards has written a story that everyone should read. It is her personal story recounted with complete and refreshing honesty and candour.

Every school child, parent, teacher and educator should have a copy of this book, and read it several times from cover to cover.

It touches the heartstrings profoundly on every page. At one level it is a disturbing and *agonizing* read, forcing reflection on the horror of child abuse in any form. It is hard to believe that any child could be subjected to the pain and abuse -verbal, psychological and physical- that the author was made to endure almost from her infancy, and that at the hands of those in whose care she was entrusted.

Her childhood experiences could have destroyed every thread of her self-esteem and self-worth, and made her grow up severely and irreparably damaged and untrusting of all adults. She could have become neurotic and self-destructive and even a vengeful social menace.

Instead she chose to channel her pain and shame into productive, enlightened pursuits to become a valuable member of society, a strong advocate of Christian values and a blessing to others, even those partially responsible for her suffering and degradation.

The book makes you angry that such inhumanity to a child is possible; you feel you want to redress the grievance; that someone ought to, in God's name.

Bullying and prejudice are twin evils with which today's youth are afflicted. Andrea's book gives a revealing insight into just how pernicious they can be, and hopefully draws attention to the plight of the many who have to endure this indignity and needless agony in silence, while the adult world, like the audiences of the Roman gladiator games, uncaringly look on as at some simple, harmless amusement.

It took courage to tell this personal story with all its ugly pathos and self-revelation, and the work needs to be rewarded with a readership that is both empathetic and responsive.

Michael White

Note from the author

*I*n 2005, the Lord spoke to me and said,
"Andréa, write down the things I have done in your life, because I want My people to know that all things are possible with Me!"

He also gave me a scripture to confirm His word:
"Publish his glorious deeds among the nations. Tell everyone about the amazing things he does." —
1 Chronicles 16:24

I was filled with awe at the unforeseeable vision, that could only be accomplished by God, through me.

I answered, "Yes, Lord."

As I began writing about my supernatural experiences, I realized that I couldn't do it without sharing some of my intimate life, so that the reader could gain an understanding of what the Lord has done in my life.

Limited by a grade nine/ten education and having learned English as my second language, I was often reminded and encouraged by the Lord along the journey that God uses all who answer His call, including unlikely candidates like me.

After rewriting my book, many times over in the last ten years, what you hold in your hands is the outcome.

I've written every page with the presence of the Holy Spirit, desiring to omit as much as possible in order to protect people—especially my family—from harm.

What you're about to read is an accurate and true—though greatly condensed—account of my life as I remember it.

I've changed some of the individuals' names to protect their identity.

And so, I submit to you my life story, with the hope that you will overlook the many transgressions, and instead come to know God's amazing and unconditional love for you!

Andrea Edwards.

"Publish His glorious deeds among the nations. Tell everyone about the amazing things He does."

1 Chronicles 16:24

To my family.... I love you forever and always.

"But you are a chosen race, a royal priesthood, a holy nation, a people for God's own possession, so that you may proclaim the excellencies of Him who has called you out of darkness into His marvelous light;"-1 Peter 2:9;

Chapter One
The Military Coup

Location: Santiago Chile, South America.
Date: September 11, 1973.

Without warning, sirens and airplanes abruptly unleashed all around us. I was in a portable classroom at school.

All of us, including our teacher, ran outside to see what was happening. Planes were flying not too far away. The teacher looking frantic, yelled for all of us to run home. None of us knew what was going on. I was only nine years old and scared, but before I went home, I needed to find my younger sister.

From the portable classroom, I ran toward the school building where she would be. As I was trying to get into the building, students were rushing out at the same time, making it difficult for me to enter.

Finally in the building, I ran everywhere looking for my sister, yelling her name. But I couldn't find her. I stumbled back outside and scouted the schoolyard until I finally saw her standing in its middle, crying in fear.

I ran to her, grabbed her by the hand, and we joined the crowds of running children. Soon, we spotted Dad in his car, anxiously waving us over; we dashed over to him and scrambled inside, and then rushed home to take refuge.

Our country was officially taken over by a military coup. From one day to another, military men armed with rifles swarmed the streets. Curfews were in place, and civilians were told to stay in their homes until further notice. We soon learned that the Chilean president, Salvador Allende, had being assassinated, and that the capital city of Santiago where we lived had been taken over by the military.

The changes in Santiago and our way of life were drastic. It seemed as if a cloud of darkness had been unleashed and Santiago had become a ghost town. Fear was etched on people's faces, and you dared not get caught in the streets during curfew; breaking the rules brought upon the death penalty. If you weren't killed, you were incarcerated and tortured. The rumor was that it didn't matter if you were a woman or a child; the rules were the same for everyone. The military showed no mercy.

As the months rolled by, curfews became more lenient, but remained in force. People were allowed to go to their places of work and education, and to do their necessary errands throughout the day, but everyone had to be back in their homes before evening curfew began.

At a certain point, a new president took over. His name was Augusto Pinochet. He was put in office on September 11 by coup d'état, effectively putting an end to Allende's democratically elected socialist government.

The military threat in the streets was very real. We heard about a hit list, and the families of those whose names were on it were all being hunted down and executed. People started disappearing at alarming rates.

According to various reports and investigations in later years, during Pinochet's regime in Santiago, thousands were killed, 80,000-plus were interned, and an estimated 30,000 women and children were tortured.

Soon we would learn that our names were on the list.

On my way to school one day, I saw a man who was getting beat up right in front of the police station. Three military men with rifles were kicking and punching the man while he begged for mercy. I looked around, signaling for someone to help him, but people walked right past, ignoring the obvious. No one intervened and I knew it was because they were afraid. I could see it in their faces. I was afraid, too, but the man's cries overpowered my fear.

Not stopping to weigh the consequences, I yelled for the military men to stop, but I was ignored.

Then I did the unthinkable.

I charged at the officers, kicking them in the legs in the hope that they would stop beating the man. One of the officers turned around with a look of shock, pointing his shotgun at me. When he saw that it was just a skinny little girl, he laughed mockingly and shook his head in disbelief as the others watched.

He walked over to me, and said, while pointing his shotgun at my face, "Run away, *ninita* (little girl), or I will shoot you!"

Terrified, I ran and hid behind their building, but quickly realized that I had just trapped myself, as there was no way out other than to walk right past the officers again. I peeked past the side of the building and saw that they were still beating the poor man. His clothes were all torn, and he was covered in blood. Since the officer's attention was on the man, I nervously tiptoed into the police station for one last chance to get the man some help.

An older, heavyset man sitting behind a desk wearing a uniform asked me what I wanted. I said, "I would like to speak to the boss."

"I am the boss!" he responded.

So I told him what his three officers were doing and the bloody state of the man getting beaten up. With a surprise reaction, he sarcastically stated,

"Si! Verdad?" (Yes! Really?) "I will go and check it out. Now, you go on your way little girl!" emphasizing his tone on "*little girl*."

I could tell his concern wasn't genuine, but he was the boss, and there was nothing else I could do.

I walked out of the building knowing the soldiers would automatically see me. I could feel my whole body shaking in fear. Nevertheless, I walked past with a posture of confidence, my head held high, displaying no fear, and I let them know that I had spoken to their boss and that they were all going to be in big trouble for beating up that man, so they had better stop!

My walk quickly turned into a run for my life, every so many seconds turning back to see if any of the military men were running after me with their pointed shotguns ready to shoot. When I finally made it to school, I threw myself on the wall, gasping for air and looking in the direction from which I'd run to see if I'd been followed. When I saw no one, I felt quite surprised that I had actually made it to school alive. I'm not so sure about the man they'd been beating up. I highly doubted that he'd survived, and he probably became another casualty of war like so many others.

Soon, Christmas arrived, and the weather was hot as it usually was in Santiago. The night sky was lit up by millions of stars, all sparkling like diamonds.

It was normally a time of celebration, when families and children in the neighborhood would come together to play and mingle in the streets until the early hours of the morning; but not this Christmas. Curfews were in place and military men stood guard with their shotguns hanging over their shoulders on every street corner, including ours, making sure that we, the civilians, stayed in our homes.

As my younger sister and I played in our backyard, we began whispering back and forth to our neighbors, the Benjamins, through the tall stone wall that separated our homes. We began to plan a way to get together, concluding that we'd have to climb over the wall. Since I was the most daring of the group, I climbed the wall carefully to see if the coast was clear.

I saw that the military men in charge of our street were standing guard under the streetlights, busy mingling with one another. I turned my focus toward my sister and reached down for her hand, completely forgetting the danger lingering behind me. As my sister reached for my hand, shots began firing. We had been spotted—or so we thought. I fell and landed on the ground beside my sister, who started crying at the sound of the gunshots, thinking that one of us had been hit. But none of us was hurt.

Believe it or not; I went over the wall by myself later, and got through carefully and unnoticed while my friends watched and waited excitedly on the other side. Once in their terrain, they showed me some of their new Christmas toys: a plastic play house and a plastic tea set to go with it. It wasn't that exciting to me as I was used to the outdoor, adventurous, tomboyish kind of fun. All the while I had to be concealed from her parents, and that was not fun. I made my way back over the wall rather quickly and unharmed.

The Christmas season was soon over, but the curfews, though less strict, remained in place.

The Beginnings

My father was born to a young mother and a wealthy older father. When Dad was fourteen years old, his dad passed away, leaving my father and his brother in charge of the home business. The older brother eventually went away to medical school and became a psychiatrist. During his youth, Dad struggled with anger, depression and fear; so much so that he was institutionalized, and diagnosed with mental illness that would be detrimental to all of us. Dad managed to finish school and become a draftsman, but even with a title, dad was a wounded man who carried his pain into his marriage.

Mom was one of four siblings born to a Chilean born father with French and Jewish ancestry who was getting known as a charismatic author. Though admired by many in his circle, Mom's father inflicted much physical abuse on her mother—and Mom witnessed it. Eventually, her father left her mother and the four children to fend for themselves, while he pursued a life of fame and women. Mom suffered much hunger and was full of fear and anger growing up. When she finished school, her plans had been to enroll in teacher's college and follow the path of others in her family, but instead she married Dad in civil court, and her teaching never materialized.

Birth

Mother became pregnant with her first child, and during her pregnancy, my father was unfaithful and physically abusive to mom. However, the child was born healthy. A year later, Mom found herself expecting again under the same abusive circumstances. Feeling depressed and completely unprepared for *me*, the second child, she tried to terminate the pregnancy. I survived and arrived in the fall of Santiago.

Mom said that all I did as a baby was cry, that I was often dangerously sick, and that I spent much of my first year living in the crib because of her depressed state.

A month after I was born, Mom got pregnant again. She gave birth to my younger sister nine months later.

School at Three

Now we were three siblings, all close in age. My younger sister and I were only ten months apart, so you can imagine how busy Mom was with the three of us. Needing a break, she enrolled me in school when I turned three, telling the teachers that I was four, the acceptable entry age for kindergarten.

I do not have any memories of my first day of school. However, I do remember Mom giving me the responsibility of looking out for the well-being of my younger sister, and so I remember *her* first day—when I was not quite four—I remember it well.

After Mom and I had tried settling my sister down in class while she cried, I was ordered to go to my class. As I sat at the very back of my classroom, all I could think about and picture in my little mind was my sister crying, fearfully. Unnoticed, I left my classroom and, sure enough, found her crying. I walked into her classroom, grabbed her by the hand, and walked out. I can clearly remember feeling completely determined in my conviction that I was taking my sister home and that no one was going to stop us.

How I managed to open the school's massive old wooden "*portones*" is a bit of a blur. However, I do remember crossing the highway while holding my sister's hand and having to help her over a concrete barrier amidst the noise of cars and horns, which I did not acknowledge. My focus was on getting my sister home where she would feel safe.

When we got closer to home, I remember feeling afraid at what Mom's reaction would be upon my arrival. Mom and Dad were both sitting outside on the terrace sipping tea, and when they saw us, they got up from their chairs quickly, looking surprised. I handed my sister over to Mom hastily, explaining how frightened she had been at school. Mom took her into her arms, and Dad looking content with me, gave my head a shake.

I later learned that it boggled the minds of both my parents and school officials as to how two toddlers had managed to get the massive wooden doors open, cross a highway unharmed, and find our way home through a neighborhood maze. God was there from the very beginnings of my life.

When I was four years old, we lived in a small house with two rooms, a kitchen, and a bedroom. The floors were unfinished, made of hard, compressed soil. I remember this house well, because it was where my first memory with sexual abuse happened.

All told, the abuse lasted only a matter of seconds, as the individual kicked me out of the bed when Mom almost caught him fondling me. I knew there was something not right about being fondled, but it was the hard kick that threw me off the bed and landed me on the cold dirt floor that enabled me to put two and two together and understand that wrong had been done to me.

When I landed, I rolled and hid under the bed in a fetal position, feeling like I had been thrown away like a filthy rag doll. The pain of rejection, fear and loneliness I felt at the tender age of four was so *real* and *hurt so much* that it pierced my tiny little heart deeply, and shifted the course of my life onto the beginnings of a dark and lonely path.

I don't remember the individual striking again, physically.

After the abuse and for years to come, I became aware of Mom's outbursts of anger towards me. I kept my distance from her as much as possible.

We moved into our new house, and a homeless man began appearing in our neighborhood, and he would expose himself to the kids playing in the streets. We would all run home scared and disgusted. He would stand in front of our house, and continue to expose himself, while he laughed like a crazy man. When Mom saw him, she would rush to close the curtains and doors of our house.

Unknown to us, the old pervert had made a barren piece of land called El Potrero at the end of our street his temporary home. He had dug a hole partly underground, and formed walls with cardboard boxes and other building materials to create a transitory dwelling.

One day, I was wandering around El Potrero with my younger sister, and we came upon this old man's place, unaware that it was his.

I went in to investigate the tiny dwelling, and suddenly, my sister who was standing outside yelled that someone was coming, and took off running, leaving me behind. As I stood with my back to the opening getting ready to exit, the old pervert suddenly charged in behind me, pushing me deeper into the hole and, like a wild, crazy man, began fondling me. Just as quickly, however, I pulled free from his grasp and ran home.

I told Mom what had happened, but she didn't believe me. Instead she called me a liar and brushed me away.

I remember feeling hurt, and afraid of it happening again.

There were other violations in my life of which I have little or no memory of, and only know because I've been told.

New Home

Dad bought a two-bedroom house in a well-to-do neighborhood in Santiago. His intentions were to add a second level with four bedrooms upstairs, since there were now four of us kids. Construction would start within the year. In the meantime, we children would share a room.

The room had a large window with a broad view of the sky which I absolutely loved. Our backyard was large, with fruit trees, a chicken coop, and a distant view of the Andes Mountains. At the very back of the yard, there was a tiny house that reminded me of a storybook house, surrounded by trees. When family came to visit, this is where they would stay.

Our property was surrounded by tall cement walls. These were not uncommon in Santiago; most homes had them for privacy and to keep intruders out. But Dad went the extra mile and cemented broken glass on top of our walls, mainly the ones in the back, to make sure no one broke in.
But although the broken glass may have kept intruders out, it was really inside the walls where danger lingered, bruising the very depths of our hearts.

Yelling, screaming, and physical fights between my parents were expected in our home. Most nights, I would lay awake in the darkness of my room in fear, counting and guessing at what number the fights would break out. When the madness was fully unleashed, sometimes they would end up in our room and in hopes of protecting Mom, I would throw myself on Dad's back, grabbing him at the neck, desperately trying to pull him away from Mom. When the fights were finally over, our house was left in shambles, our hearts in anguish, and our tiny physical bodies in a trembling state of fear, terrified of it happening again.

And it always did.

The fights didn't always happen at home; they took place elsewhere, too.

It must have been late in the afternoon as the sun was starting to settle. We were coming back from an outing, and Mom and Dad were fighting again. Dad drove right into a harbor where large ships were parked, safe from sudden ocean torrents. But as we drove in, it was revealed that we were not safe at all, as a torrent was being unleashed in the car with Dad at the wheel. He was threatening to drive into the dark ocean and kill us all.

We all screamed in fear, as Dad drove the car in the direction of the ocean. Then he suddenly stopped, turned the vehicle in the opposite direction, and drove around the harbor while he and Mom screamed at each other.

Then he once again began driving the car into the direction of the ocean, making us believe that soon we would all be drowning in its dark, terrifying waters.

The fear was too much for my little heart to bear, and I cried out in horror.

"No Daddy! Please don't kill us! I love you, Daddy! I love you, Daddy! Please don't kill us!"

The fear of dying was terrifying, and the terror seemed to go on for hours.

Finally, after much crying and pleading, Dad changed his mind and began driving home. I said,
"Thank you, Daddy! Thank you for not killing us!"

I looked at my sisters. Their faces were the very picture of terror; their look permanently chisel in my mind.

As we drove away from the bloodthirsty ocean, I began humming a tune, making up a song for Dad, to thank him for not killing us.

There was no denying that Dad could be black hearted at times, and we would all suffer the painful effects in our hearts, therefore in our way of life for decades to come.

Yet in spite of the darkness, Dad had a good side to him, and one I loved.

He was funny, and randomly made jokes that would bring laughter to my heart. I will never forget the times, though they were few in number, when Dad would tell us bedtime stories, making himself the hero in them all.

While he shared, I would try to picture Dad as my hero, shielding me from my fears.

It was in those imaginary moments perhaps, that I was able to bond a little with Dad; unlike with Mom, she was not approachable.

Guns, Chains and Metal Bars

Dad was involved in a political party, and there were times when he brought me along to his meetings. I distinctly remember one of those meetings which took place in someone's high-rise apartment building.

I sat quietly, waiting in boredom while a group of men talked politics. Then I suddenly noticed they began opening up black suitcases that were placed on the floor inside their circle. I could clearly see that the cases contained guns and rifles, each neatly within its own compartment. One of the men looked at me with concern and told Dad to take me out of the room. Dad reassured them that they had nothing to worry about as far as I was concerned, and ordered me to turn around toward the black-and-white television set.

As the meeting came to an end and we made our way home, Dad noticed that he was being followed. When he stopped at a red light, he looked nervously through his rear-view mirror, before abruptly jumping out of the car.

I followed right behind him. He went directly to the trunk and grabbed two metal bars, and when he saw me standing on the side watching him, his face revealed panic and fear. He ordered me to grab the exposed chain in the trunk.

The next thing I remember is that three angry-looking guys were heading toward us, holding metal bars in their hands, as well. The exact details after that—other than the sight of Dad swinging the bars back and forth at the men, and me trying to swing the heavy chain—are hazy, but suddenly and without warning, Dad grabbed me, threw me in the front seat of the car, and jumped in behind me.

We drove away fast, leaving the men behind.

At Dad's command, I stayed hidden while he made his escape. And he gave me orders not to say a word of what had happened when we got home. I never did.

Andrea Edwards

Unfortunate Tragedies

Not long after, I was playing in our front yard. I was swinging my younger sister back and forth on my lap while holding onto a support metal bar that came out of the top of our tall wrought-iron fence in a downward-facing forty-five-degree angle, bolted into the ground. Between each bar of the fence, there was a one-inch-wide ornamental metal bar cut to about two feet in height with sharp, pointed edges on the ends like spears. One of those sharp metal spears was bent toward the support bar I was swinging off, and as I pushed back at full force with my sister's weight on my lap, I fell back on it and was instantly impaled through my back, unable to move.

My screams were heard across the neighborhood. My sister jumped off me, confused, and my little brother came close to have a look. When he saw the pool of blood behind me, he ran into the house to get help. Mom and Dad came out running, and when they saw I was impaled by the metal spike, Dad immediately got the car running and, while everyone watched, yanked me off fast. Dad having a background of nursing, new what to do. He wrapped a towel tightly around me to stop the blood from spilling and put me in the car. As soon as we arrived at the hospital, I was rushed in and surrounded by doctors and nurses who examined and poked me.

I thought I was going to die. I kept looking at my parents for reassurance, but saw none. After some X-rays and tests were done, Mom and Dad were told that the metal spike's deep penetration had miraculously missed my heart and barely injured one of my lungs. When I heard the good news, I was simply relieved to learn that I wasn't going to die.

As I recovered over the next few days, I remember walking around slowly, feeling the pain, but life went on as it always did.

Shortly after this incident, I went to visit my aunt and her family in El Canelo in the Andes Mountains. Their place, was a paradise to me. A tropical beauty. It captured me fully.

My aunt was a high school teacher who taught in the town's local school. Their home was hundreds of years old, but beautifully kept, with large rooms, high ceilings, dark, hardwood floors, and tall windows. One of the rooms was decorated with historical pieces to the very top of the walls. In the center of the room, there were a couple of thick, long harvest tables full of interesting artifacts.

Nonetheless, as fascinating as El Canelo was, there were also dangers lurking around, like mountain lions, black leopards, poisonous creepy crawlers, big tarantulas of whom I had a few scary encounters with, and dangerous terrains. One of those dangers lingered not too far from their house. A rather large, mysterious, and desolate mud lake was close by, and entry was prohibited. The reason was obvious; if you went into the lake, you weren't coming back out. You would sink and die, never to be seen again.

So there we were, my cousin Vladimir and I, playing at the edge of the death lake, and the temptation to go in was beckoning me.

Though we had been warned of the dangers several times, I couldn't resist the evil force calling me into the lake.

So I wouldn't be found out, fully expecting to come out alive, I decided to take my clothes off, and began walking into the lake backwards so that, if I suddenly began sinking, I could run out to safety and put my clothes back on quickly. No one but my cousin would ever find out that I had disobeyed. But my plan was about to fail greatly.

I began walking into the mud lake backwards, rather fast, showing off some, when I suddenly came to a stop, unable to take another step. To my horror, I realized that I was sinking.

I panicked and began screaming for help.

Vladimir ran home immediately to get his dad, and within seconds, my uncle Alexis came running at full speed holding a rope. He threw it out to me a few times before I managed to grab a hold of it. When I finally did, I lost grip not once but a couple of times, and cried in fear, thinking I would die. When I was saved at last, I was so thankful to be on dry ground and alive.

My uncle reprimanded me with good reason, but he was unable to keep a straight face, as I fidget to hide my mud-covered body, feeling embarrassed in more ways than one.

He smiled and walked back home, shaking his head. He knew I wasn't about to try that again.

Trouble wasn't through with me yet. As we traveled back home from my aunt's house, we came across an unknown bridge that was under construction. My cousin Vladimir and I began running up the bridge, racing as fast as we could to see who would make it over to the other side first. However, we were unable to see the other side of the bridge, so we didn't know that it was unfinished and under construction on the other side and high above a busy highway.

To warn people of its dangerous condition and prevent them from falling estimating forty feet onto the highway below, there was a round metal bar at least three inches thick that spanned across two vertical bars on each side of the unfinished bridge. As I reached the top of the bridge, I could see that it curved downward and that the bridge came to an end twenty to thirty feet from where I was. I tried to slow down, but because I was running so fast, I fell on my knees on the concrete and slid all the way down, with both knees and hands working as my brakes, right to the end of the bridge. Miraculously, I hit my forehead hard on the three-inch round bar, which instantly jolted me back to a dead stop, preventing me from falling to my death.

I collapsed on the ground semi-conscious from the hard hit on the forehead, and in pain.

When my aunt saw my bloody knees, she wanted to take me to the hospital immediately. The minute I heard the word hospital, I was reminded of my recent and very unpleasant visit, and knew that was not an option for me.

I got up quickly, and began walking away from my aunt.

Letting her know that I wasn't going to the hospital.

At home, Mom and Grandmother attended to my knees the old-fashioned way. I vaguely remember a sewing needle and rubbing alcohol. However, the pain of the procedure, I remember it well.

Arica

In 1973, just a few months before the coup, we drove to Arica, the last city in the north of Chile, bordering with Peru. Mom and Dad couldn't fit the four of us kids and suitcases all into our small car the Citroneta, so Mom announced the following to the family, while I stood there listening,

"The only reason we are taking Andrea is because Grandmother will never be able to handle her *"locuras"*, meaning my craziness.

I was used to hearing mom speak negative about me, and I just ignored it. What mattered to me was that I was going on vacation and my little brother whom I loved dearly was coming too.

As we drove off to the north of Chile, the countryside was beautiful to behold. Dad shared bits and pieces of history of every town we drove through, which was fascinating to me. I thrived in listening and learning about our history. I relished every bit of information.

At nights, my little brother and I kept busy counting the stars, looking at hundreds in just one tiny spot of the infinite sky.

We finally arrived at our destination of Arica and settled in a hotel surrounded by beautiful, tall palm trees.

Andrea Edwards

The Mummy

Since Arica borders with Peru, it is known for the discoveries of ritualistic burials that had taken place hundreds of years prior, and whose findings are now in museums.

During one of our outings, we went hiking inside a cave and we reached an area where it was too dangerous to enter. Dad continued deeper into the cave alone, while we waited. After some time, Dad reappeared carrying a mummy, holding it as if he had won a prize.

When I saw the mummy, I was afraid, until Dad began sharing its possible history, and his excitement for discovering the mummy, the fear left me.

When Mom saw it though, she panicked, and demanded that Dad take it back. However, after arguing back and forth, Mom agreed to keep her with one condition: that when they got back to Santiago the mummy would have a proper burial or be donated to a museum, where many such finds already were. Dad agreed.

It was a female mummy, sitting in an Indian-style position with her legs crossed. The dry climate of the Atacama desert had helped to preserve her intact. Her head was leaning to one side and she had a thick strand of long hair with a wooden pick comb attached to it. Around

her neck hung a long leather purse like necklace, and she was covered in old, torn rags drenched in dust. As we took her back to civilization, Dad covered her in a blanket to keep her hidden.

On our way home, the well-covered mummy was on my right side and my five-year-old brother lay sleeping on my other side, in the back compartment of the car. Throughout the drive, my mind was filled with questions about her: How did she die? Was she alone and afraid when she died? I felt sad for her, having experienced the pain of loneliness and the fear of dying myself. I was glad we were bringing her back home with us. Somehow, I felt as if we were protecting her.

While my brother was sleeping soundly, I decided to play a joke on him. I uncovered the mummy's face. She was spooky looking, with sockets for eyes and all. I poked my little brother on the shoulder. When he turned around I moved and, instead of seeing me, he saw the uncovered face of the mummy.

Very bad joke! My little brother's face turned to horror, and he jumped up so fast that he hit his head on the roof of the car, screaming hysterically. He practically flew to the front seat to where Mom was, falling and banging himself in the process before landing on Mom's lap. The scare caused such a racket that Dad had to stop the car, get out, and pretend to check the back compartment to show my little brother that there was nothing there so he would calm down and go back to sleep. After yelling at me for playing such a horrible joke, Mom gave me the job of settling him down. This took a long time, as he kept looking over his shoulder to see if the monster would reappear, but we finally drifted off to sleep, counting the stars, which were shining brightly in the night sky.

Our house was being renovated. We had expanded the first level by adding two large rooms a washroom, and the second level by adding four bedrooms. Each one of us children would have a bedroom. The renovations were almost finished.

My older sister had laid claim to the bigger room upstairs and, being the oldest, she had the right. However, that was about to change because, since returning home, my sisters had taken one look at the mummy and become terrified. They wouldn't even come close to have a look.

Dad decided to take the mummy upstairs to store her.

I followed, and saw that Dad picked the bigger room, which happened to be the closest to the stairs. After a few minutes, Mom and my sisters came up and began protesting against the mummy staying inside the house at all. While the commotion went on, I thought of a brilliant idea and made a suggestion. "The mummy can stay in this room, and when the room is finished, this one will be mine."

To my astonishment, everyone became quiet and headed back down the stairs in agreement. There was still a bit of grumbling here and there, but the matter was put to rest. Officially, the big room with the big window for gazing upon the stars at night was going to be mine. I was happy as a puppy!

Mr. Benjamin

The days and weeks passed, and one evening my siblings and I were by ourselves while Mom visited with her friend. It was getting dark, and my sisters thought they could hear noises coming from upstairs where the mummy was. My one sister sent me to go and call on our neighbor, Mr. Benjamin.

Mr. Benjamin was a Christian pastor, and Dad was very outspoken about not liking Christians. Curious as to why that was, I paid extra attention to Mr. Benjamin, and found out he was different from most adults, alright, but not in a bad way. He was kind, and he always seemed to be involved with his family in a positive and harmonious way.

I went calling at his gate and explained our situation. He came over to our house without any hesitation. He began walking around from room to room, and I followed behind him. As he went, he seemed to be mumbling words as if he was talking to someone. I didn't know then, but later on, I learned that he was praying.

As we started walking up the stairs, I began getting a bit worried—not really for myself, but for Mr. Benjamin. It was getting dark, the rooms were unfinished and what would his reaction be to the sight of the mummy?

I had to say something fast. He entered the room where the mummy was sitting upright covered in an old, woolen blanket. He looked straight at it, not saying a word. For a few seconds, he was motionless, probably thinking to himself that someone was hiding under the blanket. And in fact there was a person there, only she was dead.

I quickly shared that it was a dead woman; and that we had found her when we went away to the north of Chile.

All of a sudden, Mr. Benjamin's face showed fear and shock.

Detecting by the look on his face that he must of miss understood me, I quickly explained in an anxious tone.

"Mr. Benjamin, she's *history*! As in *school history*! She could be hundreds of years old. We are going to donate her to a museum where many of them are, already, or give her a proper burial in the Andes Mountains. She is a mummy!"

He looked at me for a few seconds, digesting the information, and then finally nodded in understanding.

I was so relieved.

The Warm Glowing Light

He continued his surveillance along with his mumbling as he walked around each room. Finally, we went back to the living room where my brother and sisters were. He assured us that all was well and not to worry. Then he asked as all to gather together and he put his hands lightly on our heads and prayed for us.

While he was praying, my brother, sisters and I watched him. There seemed to be a warm, bright light all around us, and we all felt such peace.

Mr. Benjamin finished praying and went home. My siblings and I looked at each other, feeling happiness and peace like we'd never known before, and we knew that it was because of Mr. Benjamin's prayer.

We wanted him to come back and pray for us again: but *how*, we wondered. So we came up with a lie. The irony.

We would go and tell him that we were still scared when we really weren't, and then surely he would come back and pray for us again.

I called at the gate and Mr. Benjamin came out right away with a look of confusion, and said, "Yes?"

With a smile, instead of showing fear as I was supposed to, I said, "Mr. Benjamin, my sisters and I are still afraid and we were wondering if you would come and pray for us again?"

His confused look changed to a smile and he said, "Si, si." "Yes, yes."

My siblings and I gathered eagerly in the living room, staring at Mr. Benjamin with big smiles and bright eyes. He placed his large hands just above our heads again and began to pray. And there it was again: the warm, bright light of peace, surrounding us.

My siblings and I were filled with joy and peace. When Mr. Benjamin left, the warm, bright light was still with us, and my siblings and I held hands and danced in a circle around the living room, joyfully laughing out loud like never before.

From what I know now, that was God's tangible presence surrounding us.

Christian Spaghetti

Shortly after Mr. Benjamin prayed for us, I was invited over to their house for dinner. No one had intentionally invited me to dinner before. I vowed to myself to be on my best behavior.

Beatriz and Valeria welcomed me at the gates of their home with big smiles and warm hugs, and held my hands as they led me inside as if I was some important guest. I stood at the entrance, motionless, while everyone looked at me with warm smiles.

I had never been welcomed in such a kind manner before, and it made me feel a little nervous and pressured not to make a wrong move, and let everybody down.

I was asked to have a seat beside Mr. Benjamin while Mrs. Martha, along with her oldest daughter, Heidi, began serving dinner: plates filled with spaghetti. They looked delicious.

As soon as I was served, I began eating right away, but was quickly interrupted by Beatriz whisper:

"We first say grace."

Startled, I swallowed my mouthful and waited. Mr. Benjamin closed his eyes and began to pray. I looked around the table and noticed everyone had their eyes closed except for Beatriz; she was signaling for me to close my eyes, and so I did. When Mr. Benjamin finished praying, everyone began eating. I reached out to grab some bread from the center of the table, and when I pulled my hand back; my elbow accidentally hit my plate and sent the spaghetti and plate flying all over the table, all over my dress, and all over the floor.

I couldn't believe my eyes. I could literally feel my heart pounding in my throat. Things could not get any worse than they were at that very moment. All I wanted to do was run away and hide, but instead I got up with my head hung low feeling ashamed and embarrassed, and began cleaning up the mess.

To my surprise, everyone got up and began helping me. When the mess was all cleaned up, I apologized and began walking out the door, thinking to myself: Why did I have to make a mess of everything? I really wanted these Christian people to like me, and now they were going to hate me. Suddenly, my thoughts were interrupted by Mr. Benjamin's voice, speaking with excitement. *"Andrea! Where are you going? Come back here. There is lots more!"*

As I turned around, I saw Mrs. Martha coming out of the kitchen carrying another plate of spaghetti for me, and to my amazement, this plate seemed to be fuller than the last one. I couldn't believe it. My heart got filled with joy, and warm tears filled my eyes. Everyone looked at me with the same smiles they had welcomed me with.

I began eating—carefully this time—and wondered why these people were being so kind to me. In my heart I knew it was because they were Christians. And, while I ate, I desired greatly in my heart to become a Christian.

First Visit to the Christin Church

Not long afterwards I was invited to attend Mr. Benjamin's church.

I didn't really want to go because of my previous visits to the local Catholic church, that we attended once in a while. I couldn't understand anything the priest said or did, and I struggled to stay still in my seat. When I couldn't stand it any longer, I would tiptoe over to one of the confession booths and wait inside until the service was over.

So when Mr. Benjamin's family asked me to go to church with them, I sure didn't want to go. However, how could I refuse, after they had been so kind to me? And they had already asked Mom's permission, and Mom had said yes.

On our way to church, the family seemed very happy to have me on board. I, on the other hand, was dreading every minute, and plotting a way to bail out when we got to church.

We pulled into the driveway of a building that resembled a large home, rather than a church building. My first thoughts were that they'd changed their minds about going to church, and we've come to visit someone instead.

I quickly noticed that the parking lot was full of people, young and old, mingling with one another. Kids were running back and forth, laughing and giggling, seeming to have fun. I thought to myself: *This* cannot be church!

Beatriz introduced me to some of her friends, and I whispered in her ear, hoping she would say yes:

"Is this church?" "Yes," she said.

I was shocked, and wondered how that could be. There are kids running around, making noise, and having fun—*in church?*

We went into the building, and all of us kids went to another level, where we gathered together and began singing songs standing up, reminding me much of the school patriotic marches in which I participated and loved.

One of the songs grabbed my attention, and I began to feel uncomfortable as I thought everyone was singing it to me.

"O be careful little eyes what you see
O be careful little eyes what you see
There's a Father up above
And He's looking down in love
So, be careful little eyes what you see

O be careful little ears what you hear
O be careful little ears what you hear
There's a Father up above
And He's looking down in love
So, be careful little ears what you hear

O be careful little hands what you do
O be careful little hands what you do
There's a Father up above
And He's looking down in love
So, be careful little hands what you do

O be careful little feet where you go
O be careful little feet where you go
There's a Father up above
And He's looking down in love
So, be careful little feet where you go

O be careful little mouth what you say
O be careful little mouth what you say
There's a Father up above
And He's looking down in love
So, be careful little mouth what you say"

Since I was constantly in trouble with Mom, I thought maybe she had informed these people, and they had made up a song just for me. But even more surprising was that the teachers up front leading the songs didn't look upset or angry toward me at all. They looked like they were kindly and joyfully relaying the message.

Feeling convicted and yet grateful to them for going to such an extreme to even come up with a song, for me, I made a conscious choice in my heart at that moment to stay as still as possible, as my energetic behavior was the main reason for my troubles, it seemed.

After the singing came to an end, a Christmas drama presentation began.

The drama told the story of Jesus and the reason behind His birth. And as they dramatized it, I heard and understood that Jesus loved me for the first time. My heart was filled with joy and, from that day forward, I felt as if Jesus was part of my heart everywhere I went. I was nine years old.

On our way home, I couldn't stop thinking about Jesus and church. I felt happy inside, and I knew it was because of Jesus.

The next time we visited the local Catholic church, my grandmother who visited us often, came with us. This time, I paid attention, desiring to learn about Jesus. However, I didn't understand a word of what was being said, or any of the rituals the priest performed. One thing was sure: in my eyes, it didn't compare to Mr. Benjamin's church.

As we walked back home with the family, I said to my grandmother, "Abuelita ('grandmother' in Spanish),
"we should all go to Mr. Benjamin's church, instead. It's so much more fun there, and when they speak about Jesus, I can understand."
Grandma was quiet, and didn't usually answer back with words. But this time, she seemed deeply interested in my comment, because when I spoke, our eyes met and connected like they never had before. When she spoke, her response was in the form of a question, and I could see beyond her words. I could see into her heart, a searching, desiring to know more about Jesus herself.
She uttered the words, "You liked it?"
I answered, "*Me encanto*! I loved it!"
She answered pensively: "*Then we should* go…soon!"

Out of the mouth of babes God speaks

Sometime after, during a family outing, we drove past a group of Christians worshipping in the streets. This was common for Christian groups to do, and they did it unashamedly.

As we drove by them, Dad began mocking them, as he usually did. It had never bothered me before, but this time it was different. I felt as if he was mocking someone close to me, like my own family.

In an attempt to defend them, I spoke loudly, overpowering his voice.

"Dad," I said, "listen to the Christian song I learned at Mr. Benjamin's church!" And I began singing the lyrics to one of the verses.

"O be careful little mouth what you say, O be careful little mouth what you say, for the Father up above, is looking
  down in love, so be careful little mouth what you say."

When I finished singing, everyone in the car was completely silent, and Mom and Dad looked to be in deep thought, even for a long while after.

Entranced by His presence

One Sunday afternoon, my younger sister and I were playing with some neighborhood kids a few blocks away from our home, when suddenly I heard one of their mothers calling her daughter to come and get ready for church. *Church?* I thought. I want to go to church!

I asked if my sister and I could accompany them. She asked her mom, who said we should go home and ask for our parents' permission. We were a distance away, and I knew Mom would say no, because she didn't know these people. However, I was determined to go, so I pretended to run home, and hid around the corner for a few minutes, and ran back with a solid yes.

My younger sister and I walked to church with the family, and when we arrived, I recognized the building. I had walked past it many times, but never really paid much attention to it. The church resembled a large log cottage with four basic walls and large windows. When I walked in, there were people playing instruments and singing, reminding me of Mr. Benjamin's church, and the people seemed to be just as happy.

The church filled up quickly, and I got buried amongst the crowd and could no longer see up front. Not wanting to miss a thing, I walked to the front pew, which happened to be empty, and sat there, not realizing it was probably reserved for the worship team. I watched the worshipers sing and play their instrument's. Everyone in the church was singing and clapping along. I joined in, and began clapping and singing, pretending to mouth the words to the songs I didn't know. I wanted to fit in. When I noticed no one was playing the bongos in the band, I was transported in my mind to a time when Mom and Dad had been playing their Spanish folk music. I was playing our bongo drums to the rhythm of the music, and Dad proudly praised me out loud, saying,

"Everybody, look at Andrea. She can really play those bongos!"

I never forgot his affirmation, because it made me feel like I mattered. Feelings I wasn't accustomed with.

As the church continued worshiping God, I was filled with joy, so much that I began dancing around the front, entranced in the moment.

As a nine-year-old little girl who had experienced much sadness, that moment was heavenly for me.

My younger sister was also filled with joy that night and, when it was time to leave, we both stood outside the church by an old oak tree, staring at all the happy people.

We didn't want the moment to end, and to have to go home to the sadness. Nevertheless, we slowly began walking back home with the family we had journeyed with, reminiscing about what we'd just experienced.

The family began singing one of the songs we had sung in the church and my younger sister and I looked at each other as we held hands. We didn't have to express how we felt, because our smiles said it all.

The Convent

It wasn't until I learned about Jesus's love for me in Mr. Benjamin's church that the convent near our house became one of my favorite places to visit.

I thought it was the place where Jesus lived, and if He lived in it, I wanted to make it my home one day.

However, I found out that the only people who lived in the convent were priests and nuns. To be able to live in the convent with Jesus, I thought I would have to become a nun. It would be somewhat of a sacrifice, the not getting married for I liked boys and wished to be married one day, however, I was willing to give it up for Jesus.

The convent was protected with wrought iron gates and high stone walls. Inside, it looked like a paradise to me; decorated with fountains, mature trees that were perfect to climb, lush grapevines dressing the walls, saints' statues, and beautiful flower gardens. It was a place to be enjoyed, but seldom opened to the public.

Nonetheless, I visited often. I would sneak inside by climbing over the walls. Then one day, things changed rather quickly, almost costing me my life—or so I thought.

On this day, I was accompanied by my friend, Tony, who was around the same age as me, nine years old. I liked Tony because he was as adventurous as me. However, he would prove otherwise on this day.

We were climbing the stone walls of the convent as we usually did, when we suddenly heard some noise in the distance. We went to investigate. We had to be very careful as we were trespassing on private property. So, like spies, we ran from bush to bush, surveying our surroundings, and confirming that the coast was clear.

We came to a miniature house, away from all the other tall buildings. The house was partly underground, made of stone with a beautiful window. A stone staircase led down to a thick wooden door. I began walking toward it and whispered to Tony to follow me. He answered aggressively:

"You are not allowed to go in there. Only priests are allowed in there. If you go in, God will kill you!"

I was surprised at his words and the harsh tone attached to them. I had recently learned at Mr. Benjamin's church that God loved me, and if He loved me, why would He want to kill me?

Tony continued arguing his scary notion, but I didn't believe his nonsense, and decided to prove him wrong, instead.

I headed over to the little house alone, while Tony waited behind the bushes. I walked down the stairs and opened the wooden door quietly and peeped in. No one was inside, so I walked in.

The room was small. There were three small, shiny wooden pews, and an altar with a couple of statues, one of which was Jesus and mother Mary. I sat in the middle pew feeling a little nervous because, after all, I was breaking the law by trespassing on private property. Nevertheless, I looked directly at the statue of Jesus and began speaking to Him about what the Christians were saying about Him, and what Tony was saying. As I was speaking, I felt fear come over me and my body began trembling for daring to question the Almighty in such a bold manner. At the same time, with both hands on each side of me, I held tightly to the pew I was sitting on, just in case Jesus decided to smack me over the head, or hit me with a lightning bolt, or something.

But as I continued sitting there, looking toward the statue of Jesus, the fear vanished, and peace settled inside of me, with a knowing that Jesus was good.

Then suddenly I was startled by some noise coming from outside and I really got scared, because if anyone was going to hurt me, it would probably be one of the priest for daring to brake in to their prayer sanctuary.

Carefully, I sneaked out unnoticed, and jumped into the bushes where Tony was. Tony jumped up in fear at my quick and sudden appearance, probably surprised that I was still alive.

We shifted our focus to where the noise was coming from. It was a group of nuns on their way to a large building called the sanctuary. Within minutes, we could hear music coming from the building.

I began walking to the sanctuary, and asked Tony to follow me, but again he chose to stay behind, afraid to get caught.

I opened the door a nudge and squeezed in. Being skinny was one of my nicknames, and it was never used positively, but it had its advantages. Once I was in the building, I crawled and hid under a pew. The sanctuary was large, painted in light colors. There were several nuns gathered up front by the piano, singing, and their voices and the music sounded heavenly to my ears.

As I lay there under the pews, I felt such peace that I closed my eyes and began dreaming of the day I would become a nun and move into this beautiful place of peace and serenity.

I completely forgot my state of concealment.

Suddenly, without warning, the music and the singing came to an abrupt end, and I heard one of the nuns yell out something. Startled, I turned to see what the commotion was about, and noticed that all the nuns were looking and pointing straight at me. I had been discovered!

Immediately, the nuns began walking in my direction rather quickly. I crawled out from under the pews and ran out the door toward Tony's hiding place. And just when I thought I had escaped them, I turned to look back and, to my shock, saw all the nuns running behind me with every intention on catching me. Then Tony suddenly jumped out of the bushes with his hands up in surrender, looking as frightened as ever. I couldn't believe my eyes.

I, on the other hand, was determined not to get caught, and so I kept on running as fast as I could toward the climbing tree we used as our exit, which was on the other end of the convent. But every time I looked back, the nuns seemed just as determined to catch me, and as other nuns saw the commotion from other buildings, they joined in the chase as well. Then suddenly and unexpectedly I came to a dead end and was surrounded on every side, leaving me no choice but to surrender.

The nuns took me into their main headquarters and sat me on a chair. Two of them stood guard over me as one announced that she was going to call the head priest and I was going to be in big trouble. According to the nun, the priest had the powers to send me straight to hell if he wanted to.

Death flashed before my eyes. I didn't want to die, and I sure didn't want to go to hell! I had to find a way to escape.

While I sat fearfully waiting, I suddenly saw my chance. The two nuns who were standing guard over me were distracted as they conversed with one another, and the chair in which I sat was only about five feet from the double doors that would lead to my freedom. As I gained the courage to make my escape, I could feel my heart racing faster and faster, until the moment finally arrived. I jumped off the chair and charged right past the guarding nuns, and out through the double doors like a speeding bullet. I ran as fast as I could, straight to my familiar climbing tree, and jumped over the wall like a bird flying to its freedom. I did not expect the hard landing on the other side. Nevertheless, I bounced up quickly and unharmed, and ran as fast as I could, all the way home.

Back to the Coup in 1973

Soon after the coup, Mom and Dad separated, and my maternal grandmother, whom I called *"Abuelita,"* moved in with us indefinitely, mainly to help Mom in her state of depression.

My Abuelita was a well-educated lady who had studied home economics. She worked for wealthy folks as a tailor, and she was known for spending much of her free time visiting and helping the poor.

Since I couldn't go out and wander the streets as I was used to, I spent much of my time at home with my Abuelita. As I kept her company, I bonded with her like no other, and in the process, she taught me the basics of knitting and sewing, which I learned to love.

I will never forget the time when she asked me to help her skein the yarn. She made me hold my arms up while she wrapped the material around them. I maintained that pose for a long time, and my arms were starting to ache. *"Abuelita!"* I protested. *"My arms hurt!"*
She heard my cry but chose to ignore it. A few minutes passed and I repeated it, but to no avail. I withstood a bit more punishment until I just couldn't take the pain any longer and then voiced my outcry again. But, once again, Grandma ignored me. Frustrated at her silence, I gave her a mocking look of pain, and she gave me the same mocking look in return, without uttering a word. Shocked at her response, I broke into a fit of giggles, forgetting all about the pain in my arms.

Strangely, it was this back-and-forth acknowledgement that allowed me to connect with her at a deeper level. From that moment on, I looked forward to spending my time with her. But, sadly, that was soon to come to an end.

In a time in which telephones were rare in people's homes, we had other methods of communication as a family, like our own personal whistle. We used it to call or find each other when nearby, or to notify family when we went to visit them of our impending arrival.

I enjoyed whistling and could pretty much whistle any song through.

While doing research for my book, I found out I could whistle, almost as well as the international whistling champion lawyer, Harvey Pollock, from Canada.

I didn't even know such competition's existed, and contemplated of perhaps joining a whistling team myself in my adult age. But as the saying goes,

"a whistling woman and a squawking hen always come to no good ends."

So, needless to say, I keep the whistling to myself. However, that's not altogether true, as my family gets to hear an awful lot of it.

My abuelita had her own personal whistle, as well, and I remember it well this one particular day while I played in the streets. It was getting late, and she was rushing back home before curfew began. Suddenly from a distance, I heard her unique whistle, signaling to us she was near. The sound was music to my ears, and in excitement I ran toward it. When I saw her around the corner, I ran to her and hugged her around the waist, happy to have her back home before curfew. But with a sigh of pain, grandma pulled back. Her response took me by surprise.

I didn't know it then, but Grandma had been diagnosed with terminal cancer and was given a year to live, at the very most.

When the family found out about her illness, Grandma, Mom, and us kids began attending the Catholic church around the corner every Sunday morning. I began to look forward to our Sunday walks as a family.

Through this time, Mom began to lean on God, and her change was noticeable. She was no longer depressed and angry. Home was becoming a place where a sense of peace dwelled for the first time, and I knew in my heart that it was because of Jesus in our lives.

Mom wanted all of us kids baptized, as an act of faith and commitment to God, and she wanted Grandma present at the baptisms before she passed away. I was eleven years old.

Psalm 91

During Grandma's last few months, she spent most of her time in bed, and as a family we would all gather in her room and read the bible together.

Mom and Grandma had become fond of Psalm 91 and read it daily.

My Abuelita shared that whenever we felt afraid or alone, to read Psalm 91, and God would protect us.

I took that revelation to heart; so much so that I memorized the entire psalm within days, and for a period of time, wherever I went, whatever I was doing, I was reciting Psalm 91.

Eventually, Grandma became too ill to stay at home and was admitted to hospital. In October of 1976, my dear, sweet Abuelita went home to be with Jesus at the tender age of 59.

The Telegram

Weeks after Grandma's passing, Dad sent a telegram to Mom through the priest of the Catholic church that we attended, notifying her that it was urgent for them to meet as soon as possible.

Mom was grieving her mother's passing; however, she was stronger then she had ever been because of her faith in God. She agreed to see him, but her agreement came with a condition: she would only meet my father if the priest was present. She wanted to make sure that whatever it was Dad wanted, there would be a Godly accountability to lead the way for her. They scheduled a meeting at church.

Mom learned that Dad's name was on the hit list of people who were supposed to be hunted down and killed due to their political involvement. And because we were his family, all our lives were in danger. Dad explained to Mom that we needed to flee the country as soon as possible, and that he had already started procedures with the Canadian Embassy. They were ready to help us out of the country if we were willing to accept it.

Dad also promised Mom that if she agreed to come with him, we would start a new, and happy life as a family in Canada.

Mom still loved Dad, and she couldn't refuse the offer for the obvious reason: our safety. Mom and Dad, though separated, were still officially married through the civic court. But if they were getting back together,

Mom wanted to make it official before God, and get married in a church.

This is how it happened. My parents married in the church with a few family members and us four children as their witnesses.

Arrangements began immediately for us to leave the country. In less than two months, we would be moving and starting a new life in Canada, a country that I had never heard of until then. When I searched for Canada on the map, I was happy to find out that it was still in America

Beautiful Dresses

A few days prior to our departure to Canada I had a vivid dream. The dream was so real that to this very day I remember it in detail. I was in my backyard behind the chicken coop. I picked up a rock that opened up a passageway of stairs made of stones that led to a thick wooden door. I followed the path, opened the door and entered a house. The house was made of solid rock, like the house in The Flintstones, a TV show I had not yet known.

The house seemed to have many rooms, each with big windows that allowed the brilliance of the sun to shine in.

I walked into one of the rooms. The sun was shining brightly on two large closet doors. I felt drawn to go and open the doors and, as I did, to my amazement, before my very eyes hung the most beautiful dresses my eyes had ever seen. The fabrics and colors were brilliant.

I began touching and feeling them with excitement. Then as if coming from the light shining through the window, I heard a voice say,

"Andrea, these dresses are for you."

I was filled with excitement and awe.

Then I was drawn to another room, which looked similar to the first one, with a big window, and the sun shining brilliantly upon closet doors. Just like in the other room, I was drawn to open these doors. When I did, I found more beautiful dresses of brilliant fabrics, textures, and colors, and once again I heard the voice, saying,

"Andrea, these dresses are for you!"

Feeling overwhelmed with joy and gratitude, I began to touch and feel them with my fingers, and as I did, a great desire came upon me to share them with everyone!

When I awoke, I got dressed quickly, feeling the excitement of the dream. I ran to the backyard, to the same spot where the chicken coop was and where I'd found the rock in my dream. I had never really taken notice before, but the ground behind the chicken coop was covered with all kinds of small rocks. I began picking them up, one by one, hoping to find that magical rock that would open the pathway to the beautiful dresses.

I ended up spending all day behind the chicken coop looking for the rock, until evening arrived. I went to bed convinced that the rock existed and that I was going to find it.

The following morning, I got up with the daylight, and restarted my quest to find the magical rock. But once again, darkness arrived, and no rock.

How it could be? I thought to myself. The dream was so real. The rock was so real. I needed to find it, and I needed to find it fast, for our time to leave Chile was fast approaching.

I continued looking for the rock for days and weeks until I had cleared the area of all rocks.

Strange as it was, and though it had only been a dream, I knew in my heart that the magical rock existed, and I believed that I was going to find it!

"The Lord is my rock and my fortress and my deliverer"
2 Samuel 22:2;

The Vision

Nights before our departure, I lay on my bed with my window wide open, gazing up at the stars shining brightly in the royal blue sky. I began to imagine what our lives would be like in Canada, and suddenly, I began having a vision. The vision was so real. Just like the dream with the rock a few weeks prior.

I could see our home in Canada; a large log-style structure home, surrounded by the beauty of nature. The house had dark, hardwood floors. The living room and kitchen were of an open concept with large windows, allowing the sunshine in. Through the windows, I could see the tall cedars and pine trees at a distance, and their beautiful aroma filled the house.

Adorning the trees and the ground was freshly fallen snow, soft and soothing to the eye. I had my own bedroom with a big window that allowed me a grand view of the outdoors, and the stars at night which I loved watching. Our new school was only a few minutes away, which made me so happy because I could invite my new friends to my house.

When my vision ended, I was excited about moving to Canada. On my way to school, I stopped to tell the corner street vendor whom I hardly ever spoke to of our imminent departure. Kids were always stealing gum and candy from the poor old man; and that was probably the reason for the suspicious look on his face every time my younger sister and I would walk by. I cannot deny that the temptation wasn't there sometimes, but we knew better. When I finished telling the old man of our soon departure, he wished us a quick, get-out-of-my-hair farewell.

Safe to say, he wasn't going to miss us.

Departure

Our departure date finally arrived. December 22, 1976.

The airport was swarming with military men carrying shotguns. We went through serious security checks, had our fingers printed, and our pictures taken. I nervously kept my eyes on my parents, and I could see fear and worry on their faces.

They had warned us over and over before arriving at the airport not to say anything about the family if questioned, because it could get us killed. I had sworn by signaling a cross over my heart, promising not to say a word.

The hours passed and, after some time, we were informed that we were not allowed to leave the country. This was due to complications with our paperwork. I feared we were in danger.

We were placed in a high-end hotel in Santiago known to celebrities and wealthy folks while our sponsor, the Canadian embassy, dealt with the red tape. When we walked into the hotel, my attention quickly turned to the building's beautiful, rich décor. A gentleman dressed in uniform approached us, and escorted us to our room, which turned out to be two joined rooms, with large beds that were perfectly made. In front of the beds were chests of drawers with large mirrors such as I had never seen before. My little brother and I began jumping on the beds in excitement; yes, I was eleven years old. While bouncing on the bed, I glanced toward the large mirror and, for the first time in my life, saw a clear image of myself reflected back at me. I stood motionless, staring at myself. I was surprised at my appearance. Until then, all I had ever heard about my looks from Mom was negative. She would say things like I had a chicken head, or that I was too skinny, or that I stunk. But as I stood looking at myself, I didn't see the negative; instead, I felt happy, content, and even pretty. Then suddenly to the right of the mirror, I saw Mom standing on the side of the bed watching me with curiosity. When she realized I had noticed her, she harshly ordered me off the bed.

The hotel had an outdoor pool, and since I'd swum in the ocean since I was a toddler, I was a good swimmer, so I was given permission to go to the pool as long as I took my little brother with me.

We played in the water until we were exhausted. When we came out, we sat by a table to rest, and noticed that we were surrounded by people eating delicious meals.

It made us both very hungry. I knew that asking Mom and Dad for money was not an option, especially considering the trouble, I had caused days before leaving home.

Days Before . . .

I had never been given money to buy anything before, so even at the age of eleven; I didn't know the value of money. Days before leaving the house, I had come across money in Mom's dresser. I later found out it was their savings for Canada. I took a few of the bills, gathered my neighborhood friends, and took them shopping in the corner store as a farewell gift.

When the group of us entered the store, the owner who knew us looked at us with distrust in her face, wondering what kind of trouble we were up to. I quickly showed her the cash and asked her how much could we buy with what we had. In obvious surprise at the sight of the money, she said we could get whatever we wanted, and began helping us.

When I got home, I put the rest of the bills and change back where I had found it. Later that day, Mom and Dad found out, and I was punished rightfully, and labeled a thief and a liar in front of everyone. They warned me never to ask for a cent for as long as I lived.

Decades later, I learned that Mom and Dad had gone back and talked to the store owner that very same day. Given the circumstances, she had given them their money back.

Back to the Pool...

While my little brother and I sat at the pool's restaurant, hungry and shivering, a waiter approached us and said, "Would you like anything to eat or drink?"

I answered immediately.

"We don't have any money."

"Are you staying here in the hotel?" He asked with a suspicious look.

"Yes, we are." I answered.

"Well, then it's free!" he said.

My brother and I looked at each other with big smiles.

The waiter took our drink orders of two Fantas. He left us with two menus while he went to fetch our drinks. As I studied the menu with excitement, I realized that I couldn't understand any of the fancy names of the foods. So my brother and I began looking around at what some of the other people were eating. When the waiter came to take our order, we both began pointing at dishes from different tables instead, not realizing that we were ordering a few meals each. After the waiter left with our tall order, my brother and I giggled excitedly in anticipation of the food that was to come.

Finally, our waiter arrived followed by another waiter carrying trays full of plates of food. They tried to put the plates on our table, but there wasn't enough room for all of them, so we chose what we wanted and they took the rest back, looking unimpressed.

Joshua and I ate until we were stuffed, and we still hadn't even touched some of the dinner plates. After a little while, the waiter came back to clean up our table and offered us dessert.

We couldn't believe it, and though we were stuffed, we couldn't refuse. We ordered ice cream, and it arrived topped up with whipped cream and cherries. After we finished eating dessert, my brother and I literally dragged ourselves back to our room.

A little while had passed when we heard a knock at the door. Dad answered and, to my surprise, I saw a guy who looked like the waiter who'd served us at the pool, accompanied by an older gentleman wearing a suit. Curious, I stood beside Dad, but away from the view of the door, listening. I could hear Dad repeating himself saying,
"No, you have the wrong people; no one here has gone to eat at the pool's restaurant."
Dad stepped back politely, ready to close the door, but just then the waiter noticed me and pointed at me. He said in a loud voice,
"That's the girl that ordered all the meals, and she had her little brother with her!"
I panicked, and yelled back, "You said it was free!"
He yelled back, "No I didn't!"
I yelled back, "Yes, you did!"

The man standing with him turned out to be the manager of the hotel.
I had once again brought more trouble to the family. I tried to explain to my parents what had really happened, but they wouldn't listen to me. Instead,

they called me a liar and a thief, their words stinging my heart.

In their eyes, I was guilty as charged. I was not allowed to leave the room until our departure day.

After two long days in captivity, we were finally informed that our papers had been released, and that we were free to leave the country. I was so relieved!

It was December 24, and Canada would be our Christmas present.

We all traveled to the airport for the second time. There they were again: the military men standing guard, displaying their shotguns which hung over their shoulders. Fear gripped me once again. I couldn't wait until we got on the plane and flew away to Canada where we would be safe.

Some of our family members came to say goodbye. Mom and her family hugged and cried as if they would never see one another again. We finally boarded the plane, a 747 jumbo jet. My seat was by a small window, making me feel a bit claustrophobic.

Take it easy

As our plane took off, I could see our family by the large airport window waving us goodbye. We all waved back until we could no longer see them. Suddenly, we flew into the clouds, and Santiago vanished out of sight. Soon, Canada would be on the horizon.

The plane had a large movie screen for us to enjoy, and the movies playing were apparently in English with Spanish subtitles. I listened attentively to the English being spoken, and tried hard to understand it, but I couldn't make out any words.

I asked Dad, "Is English difficult to learn?"

He answered, "No, not at all. To speak English, all you have to do is add the letters I, O, and N to the end of every Spanish word. If no one understands you, you simply say, 'Take it easy.'"

"Take it easy" were our first official English words.

Of course Dad was not really serious about adding and I, O, and N to every Spanish word, but it sure kept me busy throughout the flight—until we encountered some serious trouble.

As the plane flew above the Andes Mountains, we began experiencing some mild turbulence, which quickly turned to strong turbulence, shaking the plane.

I became frightened. Then when we thought it couldn't get any worse, it did. The plane suddenly seemed to be losing altitude, and we were now plummeting—plummeting to our death, I thought!

People began screaming and crying; their faces beset with fear. We were informed that turbulence was the culprit and, under the grim circumstances, that we could retrieve the paper bags if we felt like vomiting. I couldn't believe these people were more worried about keeping the plane clean than the fact that we could all die.

At any rate, vomit I did, everything I had eaten at the hotel days prior; all over the small paper bag, all over me, and all over the floor. I thought for sure we would all die before we even got a chance to see Canada.

After experiencing what seemed like a lifetime of terror, the plane stopped plummeting, and we were all somewhat relieved. Nevertheless, turbulence continued shaking the plane throughout the flight, and I kept my eyes glued on people to see if we were going to survive this flight from hell. This wasn't helpful, as everyone had fear and uncertainty carved onto their faces. Eventually, I dosed off, waking every so often to survey my surroundings before slipping right back into unconsciousness, which was better.

₷Chapter Two₷
Canada

Suddenly, I was awakened by the excitement of our imminent landing in Canada. We were flying into the Pearson International Airport in Toronto, which was not our final destination of Alberta.

It was dark, and hard to see out the window, but as the plane flew closer and closer, the City of Toronto appeared in sight, and it shone like a Christmas night! And so it was, Christmas Eve in Canada.

From the Toronto airport, we headed to our destination of Edmonton, Alberta.

The Edmonton International Airport, wasn't as lit up as the Toronto airport, and that's because the airport was located outside of the city.

I was so excited when we finally exited the plane and walked into the airport, until I noticed the incredible similarities to Santiago's airport. A sudden fear came upon me, thinking that perhaps we were still in Chile. I quickly surveyed my surroundings to see if there were any military men, and I was relieved to find that there were no signs of them anywhere. The only signs were those of Christmas decorations. We gathered our suitcases and followed Dad as he went to hail a taxi.

Outside the airport, the snow was piled up like miniature mountains on every corner. I was instantly taken back in thought to a once upon a time when I had hoped to never see snow again. . . *As a family, we had driven to the south of Chile up to the Andes Mountains for the purpose of seeing snow, something we'd never seen before. When we finally reached the very top of the mountain, Dad went to park, but when he tried to stop, the car slid, and didn't come to a stop until part of the car was hanging over a precipice. All of us began screaming and crying in a panic, thinking that the car was going to fall hundreds of feet, and we were all going to die. People began gathering around us looking for ways to help. Some men helped Mom and Dad out first while others held the back of the car so it wouldn't slide down the precipice. With much caution, my siblings and I were ushered out to safety; and the car was saved, too.*

I stood by the large window looking out at the snow and observing the surroundings, and I was happy to see no signs of precipices anywhere. Just small snow hills piled up everywhere, looking very inviting.

We were still wearing our summer clothes, since Chile was in summer bloom. Without giving my inappropriate clothing—a short, sleeveless mini dress—any thought, I charged through the doors, headed straight to one of the snow banks, and jumped and rolled on the fresh falling snow, getting covered from head to toe, relishing the moment.

However, as you can imagine, my excitement was short-lived in my summer dress. Within seconds, I began shivering uncontrollably. Never had I experienced such cold. Mom got busy opening up suitcases to find us adequate clothes to wear. She handed me my winter coat, which they'd bought before leaving Santiago; for weeks, I had looked forward to wearing it. It was bright red, made of real wool with white fur around the sleeves.

We all quickly jumped into a taxi and headed to our destination, the Kingsway Hotel. I shivered all the way to the hotel, and every so often I would ask out loud why my winter coat wasn't working yet.

It was well past midnight when we drove into the parking lot of the hotel, so it was officially Christmas Day. Across the street from the hotel, I noticed there were nightclubs, taverns, and people staggering from place to place, as if they were drunk. A man was passed out on the sidewalk, and there was a crowd of people yelling and fighting in the middle of the street. My mouth dropped in disbelief. I asked Dad why there were people fighting, and why a man was sleeping in the cold street. Ignoring my question, Dad quickly turned our attention toward the hotel, which was nothing like I had imagined. They looked like cardboard boxes with doors and windows. I was use to Santiago's colonial style. 19th century neoclassical, neo-gothic architecture. Feeling disappointed, I asked Dad if this was going to be our home.

"Only until we find a house," he said.

I was relieved.

We walked into our hotel. In the middle of the room sat an old checkered couch that had seen better days. I ran to open a double set of closet doors in the same room, and I was surprised to see long metal bars running across, horizontally and vertically. We all gathered in front of it, trying to figure out what it was. Dad began tinkering with it and, after a few minutes and to everyone's amazement, the whole thing began coming down over our heads. To our surprise, it turned out to be a perfectly made bed. Laughing out loud, I jumped on it, and said,

"Wow, Canada has beds coming out of closets! How about that!"

I ran down the hallway and came across the washroom. I was fascinated by the new bathtub, just like the one at the hotel in Santiago, attached to the floor, unlike ours back home which had feet. I turned the beautiful crystal faucets and, to my amazement, cold and hot water began pouring out of them. Back home, if you wanted hot water for your bath, it was a forever process of having to boil the water. Most of our showers were cold, and that was fine in the summer, but not so fine in the winter.

I yelled for everyone to come and see my new discovery, and announced to all that, since I had been the one to discover it, I was claiming the first bath.

Though it was late, I spent at least an hour in the hot bath, floating and relaxing; and every time I felt a slight chill, voilà, I turned on the hot crystal faucet and more hot water would pour out. When I finally came out, I noticed that my skin, especially my hands and feet, had actually shriveled up like wrinkled prunes, and my skin appeared to be as white as the Canadian snow.

Feeling a little concerned and wondering if my skin was going to dissolve away like a lump of sugar in a cup of tea, I dried up quickly, got dressed, jumped into bed, and hid under the covers, not wanting any one to see me. If it was bad news, I didn't want to hear it. Every few seconds, I would find the courage to pop my hands from under the sheets to see if my skin was going back to normal; I was relieved to see that it was.

The following morning, I woke up filled with excitement, announcing to everyone that it was Christmas Day in Canada! I got dressed, and rushed outside to see Canada in daylight.

Miniature snow banks were piled up high in every corner, just like at the airport. We climbed them and slid down, but the fun of that came and went quickly.

Looking out the window from one of the hotels was a girl who looked to be about my age, and every time I would stare in her direction, she would hide behind the curtains, and then in a little while, reappear.

The next time she did, I waved hello, signaling for her to come and play with us, but she quickly disappeared before reappearing with the head of a doll whose hair she began brushing.

In shock and disbelief, I wondered who could have done such a wicked thing as to cut her doll's head off.

I didn't know that in Canada, dolls' heads were actually sold for the purpose of playing hairdresser.

Feeling sad for her, I signaled for her one more time to come and join us; but she disappeared again, and I never saw her after that.

We were quickly enrolled in a school and placed in a regular English classroom. While the students worked on their studies, I was given children's picture cards with English words I couldn't understand or read. Some of the students stared at me, some with mocking looks, making me feel embarrassed and even dumb.

Back home, I'd liked school, and managed to get fairly good grades; however, I realize quickly that this was not going to be the case here. Also adding the letters, I, O, and N to the end of every Spanish word as Dad had mentioned, was not English.

Lunch time arrived and everyone rushed out of the classroom. My younger sister and I followed the crowds, not really knowing where we were going. We arrived at the gymnasium where everyone sat on the floor and began eating their lunches. Mom didn't know how everything worked, I guess, so she sent us without a lunch, probably thinking that the school was going to feed us lunch, as it had back home since Dad had left. She soon found out and packed us a fruit and a drink, which wasn't enough, because I was still starving.

I watched everyone eat their lunches, and was surprised to see that many of the students would throw their untouched lunches into the garbage bin. In all my life, I had never seen food thrown away, but it gave me an idea. I waited until everyone was gone from the gymnasium, and quickly pulled unopened foods from the garbage can for my sister and me to eat. But that soon came to an end, as the custodian was usually cleaning up at the same time the kids were exiting the gym, and his eye was on us.

Back at the hotel, we could hear and see the people across the street in the club and tavern yelling and fighting every night. I had seen my fair share of fighting and was not unfamiliar with it, but as far as I was concerned, we had left all that behind. I never wanted it to be part of my life again for as long as I lived.

Most recesses and lunch hours, I would stand by the heater at the entrance of the school door to keep warm, and wonder why my new coat wasn't working. Dad would say it was only a matter of time before I got use to the cold.

In one of those lunch hours, a few girls from my class stood just a few feet away from me in a group, talking. I was listening attentively, trying to understand and see if I could pick up any words, but the English language sounded nothing like Spanish. Then one of them suddenly turned to me and said something, followed with an expression on her face as if expecting an answer back from me. I answered in Spanish.

"No te comprendo," I said. It meant: "I don't understand you."

I was hoping that maybe she would understand me.

She said something else that rang a bell, but I still couldn't understand, and was reminded of what Dad had said on the plane:

"If they don't understand you, just say,

'Take it easy.'"

I did just that.

The girl looked at me somewhat shocked, with her head tilting back and forth. Her face turned to a smile that quickly turned to a frown that turned into a mocking look, followed by the same word she had been repeating all along: "Stupid!"

I thought about it for a moment, and suddenly understood. She was calling me "*Estupida!*" In Spanish, it was written almost the same. Then to my surprise, she mockingly began repeating herself over and over again, and her friends joined in, laughing. Feeling shattered, I looked outside at the cold grey sky while the girls continued their insults.

I told them off in Spanish, and then walked out into the cold. I stood outside, as tears filled my eyes, shivering and thinking that Canada was feeling a little too cold for me in more ways than one.

We soon transferred to Sacred Heart Catholic School, which offered English as a second language. My sisters and I began getting harassed immediately because we couldn't speak English. One day when I was walking out of the school, my younger sister was being pushed around by three girls who were much bigger than us. I ran toward them, yelling in Spanish in my sister's defense. Startled, they stopped and quickly turned against me. I yelled for my sister to run home, hoping to run away with her, but by then, my sister was a good block away, and I was surrounded.

Trying to find a weapon of intimidation and not being able to speak English was almost impossible. I had to think fast, and was instantly reminded of the yelling of one of my family members when they got angry. It was loud, and scared everyone. I would do the same. I began yelling just as loudly. The girls looking scared, turned around, hurrying to pick up their school bags and run away as fast as they could. They looked like they had seen a ghost.

I stood with mouth wide open in shock, and relief that my madness had actually worked.

After that incident, every time I came across the same girls in school, they would purposely look away or lower their heads to avoid making eye contact with me. This gave me a false sense of security, thinking that behaving crazy and tough would actually protect me from getting hurt.

But what was really happening was that I, Andrea, had begun to retreat into a prison of fear within myself, and a lie began to control my thinking, my emotions, and my actions; a lie that would keep me captive for years to come.

Jeans

We moved from the hotel to apartment buildings and transferred schools for a third time. St. Catherine Junior High was right across from our apartments. Fear and anxiety gripped me. I really wanted to fit in and make friends.

Right off the bat, I took notice that almost everyone in school wore blue jeans, and I thought that if I was going to fit in and have friends in Canada, I had to get me a pair of blue jeans. I begged Mom to buy me a pair. But her answer was a solid no, with a long reminder of my previous sins just before leaving Chile. I sat on the edge of my bed moping, predicting my horrible future in Canada. The odds were against me; I couldn't speak English, and my clothes were out of style.

Suddenly, I was instantly catapulted from my negative thoughts when my little brother walked by wearing my lifesavers: GWG jeans! Since arriving in Canada, Mom had gotten a job at the GWG jean factory, and had brought home a couple of pairs of jeans for my little brother, who was four years younger than me. When the house grew quiet and everyone went to sleep, I tiptoed to my brother's room, took his jeans, and went to the washroom to try them on.

The washroom mirror was small and sat high above the sink, so I got up on top of the toilet seat, which was right across from the mirror.

I could see myself from about my knees up, and to my amazement, my brother's jeans fit perfectly on my skinny frame. They were a little snug and a few inches too short, but I thought to myself: Who is going to notice such a minor thing anyway? I was about to find out.

The following day, I walked down the hallway of the school, feeling like I was finally part of the crowd instead. But the moment was short-lived. A group of girls from my class happened to be walking right behind me when suddenly they began laughing out loud in front of everyone, pointing at my jeans, making gestures about how short they were. I was crushed.

As the days rolled by, depression hovered over me like a dark cloud. I longed to be back in Chile and surrounded by the beautiful nature I so loved. Here in Canada, where was I to go, in the dead of winter?

//Andrea Edwards

Ruby

One lunch hour in the schoolyard while I stood outside shivering from the cold, I noticed a girl who, like me, was always alone. She walked with a noticeable limp.

For some strange reason, I felt as if we had something in common as I watched her. No friends, no jeans, and we both had a limp—only mine was unseen, a wound in my heart that I was desperately trying to fill by trying to fit in. With my very limited English and using hand gestures, I got the courage to befriend her.

Her name was "Ruby"—spelled "Rubi" in Spanish, and meaning the same. As a lover of stones, the ruby happened to be one of my favorite stones. My paternal grandmother always wore a ruby ring, and every time I saw her, I would reach out for her hand just to admire the precious stone.

I had never met anyone named Ruby before. When I heard her name, my thought was that her parents must really love her to have named her after such a beautiful and precious stone. I didn't understand it then, but within me I was longing for my parents' love.

Ruby's hair was long and reddish as her name, and she had beautiful blue-green eyes which were hidden behind thick glasses.

As our friendship grew, I learned she was in the same grade as me, but in a different class.

One day, she invited me for lunch at her place, which was in one of the brick apartment buildings opposite the school. She lived with her mother, her stepfather, and her birds—of whom she was very fond—that flew freely around the house.

I couldn't understand her living arrangements (not the birds flying freely—I thought that was the neatest and kindest thing I'd ever seen—but the presence of another man who wasn't her father living in the house with them.

As I visited with her, I began thinking what would happen if her real dad walked through the front door and found the other man living in the house with them. Surely all hell would break loose, just like it used to in our house when Dad accused Mom of having other men, which was never true.

Fearfully, I kept an eye on the front door, and watched Ruby for signs of nervousness. But she didn't look worried at all. Instead, she was chatty and seemed remarkably happy to have me as her company. Nevertheless, I decided to leave, just in case. I didn't want to be part of the chaos.

Another lunchtime, Ruby invited me to go and have lunch at her real father's house, which happened to be only blocks away from the school. He lived in a small, cozy basement apartment. We sat in his kitchen while he joyfully prepared us lunch. I thought it was strange for a man to be doing the cooking. In my culture, that was women's work. He had gained my respect. However, the food was another story. I had never seen such a dish like it before. He put a piece of bologna on each plate, and then opened a can of corn and put some on top of the bologna. Then, on top of the corn, he put a fried egg. He served us the dish. I was afraid to eat it, but to refuse to eat was disrespectful in our culture. You always eat what is put before you—unless it was zucchini or cooked onions (these two food's I did not eat!). Ruby joyfully poured ketchup on her food and offered me some. I had never tasted ketchup before either, so I apprehensively poured a few drops on the side of my dish and slowly began eating the strange combination.

To my surprise, the food tasted pretty good and, with delight and hunger, I finished it all.

Although Ruby and I had become friends, we both seemed to be outcasts in school. I thought it was because we didn't own a pair of jeans, and I was going to fix that.

Not realizing that it was because I had a void in my heart that I was desperately trying to fill.

One day after school before my parents got home from work, I went snooping for money in their bedroom and came across Mom's cigarettes, instead. I took one to my room, lit it up, and, as I inhaled, began coughing and choking from the smoke. I thought I would die in the process. After recuperating, I went back looking and found an envelope with money. I quickly took a few bills, and headed over to Ruby's house.

I showed her the money and asked her to take me somewhere to buy a pair of jeans, promising to buy her a pair, as well. At the sight of the money, Ruby's face lit up. That was a good sign, assuring me I had enough.

We went to the Army Navy Store downtown. The building looked like a huge factory with two levels. I followed Ruby upstairs to where the women's clothes were, and we began shopping. We both grabbed a few pairs of jeans and shirts and took them to the dressing room to try them on.

We were having so much fun trying on clothes, modeling them back and forth, that our laughs and giggles carried on throughout the store.

Once we were done, we both picked and bought the exact same tight jeans with zippers on both hips, and the same matching navy blue silk shirts, with tiny silver stars as their pattern. We took our things to the cashier and I held out the money in my hands for Ruby to sort out what we needed. I looked toward the cashier, and she looked back at us with a look of suspicion, as if she knew the money was stolen. I was flooded with guilt and began to panic. I gave Ruby the money and rushed off. She paid and then desperately began limping behind me, trying to keep up. Suddenly, to my disbelief and horror, Ruby began yelling my name out loud, repeating it over and over again, saying, "Andrea! Andrea! Stop rushing! Why are you rushing? Why?"

I froze in the middle of the stairs, afraid to look back, waiting for her to catch up and hoping she would shut up.

When she finally reached me, she insisted on knowing why I was rushing. Feeling panicked, I whispered, "I have to go home!"

"Well you could have told me!" she answered, loud enough for everyone to hear.

As we continued walking down the stairs and out of the building, I felt that everyone who stared at me did so because they knew I was a thief, and that the police had been notified and were on their way to arrest me, lock me up, and who knows what. Talk about paranoia!

My panic was obviously brought on from having experienced the military coup.

When we finally walked out of the building, I was so relieved. But it wouldn't last for long.

When I got home, I hid my clothes and put whatever money I had back in the envelope.

Morning came and Mom and Dad left early for work, as usual. I put my new clothes on and left to meet Ruby.

When I saw Ruby walking toward me wearing her new clothes, her limp seemed less noticeable, and she had more of a confident look about her.

As we entered the school, everyone appeared to be looking at our silky blue shirts with silver stars and new jeans with silver zippers on each side. We literally resembled two Nashville country singers ready to perform.

The two girls who had previously laughed at my short jeans approached me right away and pulled me aside, wanting to talk to me but not to Ruby. I didn't want to leave Ruby alone so with my limited English, I said, "Ruby is my friend. She stays."

But they insisted that they needed to talk to me alone. Ruby decided to leave on her own, and she walked away with a sense of dignity and pride (but I could see the hidden pain in her countenance, which made me feel sad). Wasting no time, one of the girls said,

"Andrea, you know how every morning when you come into the classroom the teacher asks you,

'How are you today?' And you answer him, 'I am five?'

"And the teacher says, 'No, not five. Fine.'"

"Jes," I answered. "Yes."

"Well, we will teach you a better word to say to the teacher. A nicer and much easier word that will make the teacher very happy with you. When the teacher asks you,

'How are you, Andrea?' You answer him, 'F*** you!'"

After they spent a few minutes teaching me the word, repeating it over and over again, they left for class, encouraging me to practice before entering the classroom.

When I walked into class, I immediately noticed the girls who had taught me the new word to my left, already sitting at their desks along with the other students in the class. They all seemed to be focused directly on me, wearing big smiles.

The teacher approached me and asked his usual question:

"How are you today, Andrea?"

Expecting him to be proud of my new English word, I said. "F***you,".

The whole class began laughing hysterically, except for the teacher; he didn't look happy. At all. Signaling toward the door, he walked over to me, spun me around and pushed me out of class and all the way to the office, where he forcefully sat me on a chair. Then he walked over to the secretary, said something to her that made her give me a dirty look, and walked away, shaking his head. Confused and frightened, I sat waiting, not understanding what was happening. In a little while, a girl from school who spoke Spanish came into the office, sat beside me, and asked me why I had sworn at the teacher.

In shock, I answered, "I didn't."

She told me that apparently I did, and that now I was in trouble.

I was called into the principal's office accompanied by my translator and warned about what happens to students who swear at teachers. He opened up his desk drawer, pulled out a black leather strap, and smacked it on his desk, making me jump in fear. Even though I had declared my innocence, the principal didn't believe me, and I was made to promise that I wouldn't do it again.

My parents were informed of my bad behavior at school. When I got home, double trouble awaited me, as they had also discovered the missing money. My new clothes were taken away from me. I was punished and threatened to never ask for a cent as long as I lived.

¿Chapter Three?
The Good, the Bad and the Ugly

I was glad when summer arrived, but I was not thrilled when Mom notified us that we were enrolled in English classes for the summer holidays. If anything, I thought I needed a break from the Canadian school system already. Nevertheless, good was to come from it.

Our first day in class we became friends with classmates who were siblings. They had recently arrived in Canada from Arica, Chile. I was familiar with Arica, having visited the city only three years prior. It was the place where we had found the mummy. I was happy to have found friends I could interact and mingle freely with in Spanish.

Soon, our new friends invited us to a Spanish youth service at a Christian church. When we arrived, we were introduced to a group of Spanish youth. We all came together and began singing Christian songs I had never heard before. After the singing ended, the youth pastor began speaking about Jesus and His love for us, and joy filled my heart, taking my mind back to the first time I had visited Mr. Benjamin's church in Santiago, on Christmas three years earlier. It had been the first time I had heard someone say that Jesus loved me, and when I heard those words, I felt His love and joy tangibly in my heart. It was just like I was feeling it now, here in Canada, amongst these Christians whom I had just met.

I knew I had found a place where I belonged.

When the service ended, the youth pastor and his siblings gave us a ride home, and they all followed me up to the apartment to introduce themselves to my parents.

I knocked at our apartment door with the crowd of Christians standing behind me. Unaware of the crowd, Dad came to the door barely dressed with a beer in one hand and a lit cigarette hanging from his mouth. Startled at the crowd standing behind me, he immediately closed the door in our face, saying,

"Perdon. Ya vuelvo!"—"Pardon me. I'll be back!"

After a few minutes, Dad returned and opened the door again. He apologized for his appearance and welcomed everybody in. The Christians kindly introduced themselves to my Mom and Dad and stayed long enough to invite them to church on Sunday. When my parents agreed to attend, I felt such joy that I began jumping up and down in excitement, because I truly believed *Jesus* was what our family needed to be happy.

We began attending church faithfully as a family every Sunday, and my sisters and I began attending youth activities throughout the week.

The youth pastor and his siblings would take it upon themselves to pick up a group of the youth on their way to church during the week. The crowd consisted of at least ten of us all packed in one car. We were squished like sardines in a can—minus the odor, of course, as the Spanish loved lathering on the cologne and perfume.

Once inside the car, we couldn't move an inch, sometimes making it hard to breathe. Afraid of being squished in the middle, I always managed to stick close to the window.

Every time we came to a stop, people in other cars would stare at us dumbfounded, some of them even giving us the evil eye and shaking their heads, probably thinking to themselves: Look at this pathetic sight of hooligans looking for trouble!

Of course they'd probably never suspect that we were actually on our way to church to pray for their salvation. Thank God it was in the day when seatbelt laws were not yet enforced, and packing ten-plus people in a four-door car was not illegal. Some of those cars from the seventies were nicknamed "big boats" for a reason.

Getting out of the vehicle was hilarious for those watching, and we always giggled and laughed throughout the process.

As our youth group grew larger, we started a youth chorus. I joined and began learning all kinds of Christian songs that would stay with me for a lifetime.

When summer arrived, the church planned a two-week family camping trip. My family came along. We played sports and games. At nights, we sang songs by an outdoor fire.

The youth found a great place to swim away from the adults.

Since I didn't have a bathing suit, my friend let me borrow a bikini. When I put it on, I noticed it hardly covered anything on my slim but developed body. I knew it was going to be a challenge to get to the part of the river where the youth were swimming, as I had to walk past the area where the older crowds were swimming, and I knew my swim attire—or lack thereof—would be a problem in a strict religious setting, as it was.

I ran by the adults quickly, when suddenly I heard a lady yelling Mom's name. She said,

"Your daughter is practically naked!"

I froze in the moment, watching Mom looking at me in horror and disbelief and rushing out of the water toward me. I knew if I waited, I would be sent back to change, and wouldn't be allowed to go swimming. So I took off running like the Road Runner, through the bushes and trees which led to the other side of the river, and jumped in the water, submerging myself for as long as I could hold my breath. When I came up for air, there was no sign of Mom. But on my way back, there she was, waiting on the path, and before I could cause any more upset, she took me to remove the "threads," as she called them.

Though I couldn't go swimming anymore, I loved everything about living out in the woods, from the cozy feel of the log cabins to the daily church services when we came together as a family and praised God in unity. Though I had only known these Christians just over a year, I felt as if I had known them all my life. They were my family.

In one of the church services, a message really stood out to me. The pastor mentioned that Jesus, who is God, didn't even have a pillow to lay His head on, sometimes.

I remember feeling so sad for Jesus. I couldn't imagine not having a pillow to sleep with. When the lights went off in the cabin, I lay hugging my pillow, feeling grateful to God for it and, at that very moment, Miriam, our youth leader, asked me if I could close the night with a prayer.

I had never prayed before, but I felt honored to talk to Jesus. When I closed my eyes, I could see a picture of Him sleeping without a pillow, and thus my prayer began,

"Dear Jesus,"

"I am so sorry that You never had a pillow to sleep with. I want to thank You for my pillow. And I thank You that everyone here has a pillow to lay their heads on."

Suddenly, two girls began laughing, mocking my prayer. Startled and confused, I became silent. Miriam spoke up with authority, rebuking the girls.

She said,

"How dare you laugh and mock when someone is praying. Andrea's prayer is true; Jesus didn't even have a pillow to lay His head on. We should be thankful like Andrea is for everything we have, including our pillows. Now be silent and have reverence when someone is praying."

She then asked me to continue praying. Out of respect for Miriam, I finished my prayer, but I kept it short, feeling the waves of intimidation.

McCauley School

Shortly after our church camp, we moved from the apartment building to a two-story condominium in the north of Edmonton. I transferred schools to McCauley Junior High, which was still situated in the downtown area. The school was a three-bus tour to and from, so we were often late.

I played basketball in my gym class. I loved the sport and the fact that I didn't need to speak English to participate.

I had never played the sport before, so I mostly learned the rules and regulations by watching and making mistakes.

My gym teacher was also my homeroom teacher. She was kind, and praised me when I did well, something I wasn't used to. Her praise encouraged me to want to do better.

I was so happy that school was starting off right for a change; but, sadly, that was all about to change—and drastically.

Later in the season, I learned that we would be playing basketball tournaments, and that we would sometimes be traveling to other schools after school hours, which meant that I would be arriving home late on those days. I tried to communicate the procedure of the tournaments and the urgency of my participation to my parents, knowing that I otherwise could no longer be part of the team. However, before I could get halfway through my sentence, the conversation was over, and a solid "no" was the answer. My parents zeroed in on the words "game" and "arriving home late," and assumed that I was lying. They didn't give me their permission or allow me to mention it again.

I was devastated. I didn't want to let my teacher and team down, and I couldn't muster the courage to tell them my news. So I continued playing, and when the tournament days arrived, my stomach ached all day just thinking about the trouble I would be in when I got home.

When I walked into the house, my parents stopped whatever they were doing and came charging at me, yelling, hitting me, and accusing me of being somewhere else other than school. They gave me no chance to speak in my defense. Once they were done with me, I was sent to my room until I was called down to eat.

I continued going to the tournaments, and the madness continued when I got home.

Around the same time, a school ski trip was approaching and we were given permission forms to bring to our parents to sign. I gave the form to my parents. They looked at it quickly and seemed not to have any difficulty with it, until they saw the required payment. I wasn't allowed to go. The reason? Because of the money I had previously stolen for the jeans and the money back home before leaving. I begged them to change their minds, but the answer was still no.

The week of the ski trip arrived, and everyone in the class was excited about going. A girl named Tina from my class asked me if I was going. I said no. She stated that everyone was going, and asked me why I wasn't going. I said I didn't have the money. Then she offered to ask her Mom for the money so that I could go. Surprised at her offer, I accepted. After all, the issue with my parents was the money.

When we arrived at the ski resort, the place was packed with students from all different schools. One teacher was yelling out announcements to all the students that I didn't understand, but learned later that there was a designated area for ski beginners to go before hitting the slopes.

Tina and I got fitted with our skis and headed outside.

I looked toward the ski hills, and watched the people skiing down the mountains, sliding from side to side, having fun. By the looks of it, it seemed easy enough, I thought.

We climbed into a chair lift and up we went.

Tina and I were so excited, giggling back and forth. I was so happy to have found a new friend who cared enough to even pay for my trip. When we finally arrived at the top of the hill, I came out of the chair lift feeling the excitement.

I threw myself down the hill in confidence, and began gaining speed, rapidly.

Suddenly, I realized my speed was out of control, and that I didn't know how to slow down or come to a stop. In a panic, I began yelling and signaling for people to move out of my way as I passed them like a speeding bullet. I was desperately crying out for someone to help me stop, and those who saw my distress tried showing me moves, twisting their bodies sideways. But I didn't understand what they were doing.

I saw a young man who, by the looks of his attire, worked there. Noticing my distress, he began waving his hands to me and mimicking the same moves the people I was passing were. I quickly put two and two together, and figured out it meant "stop."

But by now it was too late. I was heading right toward a mesh fence at full speed. In sheer panic, I tried imitating the move sideways but, instead of coming to a stop, I went flying in the air and tumbled around, twisting tendons and breaking joints. I came to a stop at the bottom of the hill, screaming in excruciating pain.

People began gathering around me. The young man tried pulling one of the skis out from between my legs, only intensifying the horrible pain. After some time, a few men picked me up and carried me to my teacher's car which drove me down the mountain. Words cannot express or even describe the physical pain I endured through that process. Only those who have been through it know. After enduring even more excruciating pain while the doctors and nurses put my legs back together in bandages and a cast, I was notified that my parents were on their way to the hospital.

I was afraid, because I knew trouble awaited me. When Dad arrived by himself and saw my injured state, he smiled empathetically and said,

"You see what happens when you disobey your mother and me. God punished you. Next time, it will be worse."

As Dad carried me into the house that night, Mom repeated his exact words.

The Visit

Shortly after the accident, the teacher and the girls from the basketball team came to see me at home. They had telephoned my parents throughout the week to inform them of their surprise visit. Mom decided to tell me anyways, warning me not to say anything about the fights at home. I promised I wouldn't say a word for fear that they would take the visit away from me.

When I saw the teacher and the entire basketball team at the door, it was still a great surprise. My teacher was kind and funny, at least from what I was able to pick up when she spoke. She addressed my parents, with me as the translator, which was not helpful. She boasted about how good a basketball player I was, and how much they missed having me on the team. My parents smiled emphatically, but I knew her compliments meant nothing to them. Mom said to me in Spanish—wearing smile—that it didn't matter to her that I was doing well in sports. Her desire was that I become a professional—a professor, a doctor, someone important so that she could be proud of me one day. Not a basketball player. She then wanted me to let the teacher know that they were grateful for her visit, but that they had things to do, hinting that the visit was over.

After the visit, I couldn't wait to get back to school, not knowing that things were about to get even worse.

A few days after returning to school, on my way out of the washroom I noticed a group of girls harassing a smaller girl who looked to be a recent immigrant. She looked frightened and couldn't speak any English. I walked over to stand beside her and, with my limited English, told the girls to leave her alone. One of them swore at me, and I swore right back the swear word I had been taught. The next thing I knew, we were in a fight, rolling down a concrete set of stairs, pulling at each other's hair. A few teachers broke us up, and we were taken to the principal's office where we both got in trouble. We were made to sit across from one another just outside the office.

Since returning to school, no matter how much I'd tried to keep away from trouble, it found me. Whenever I saw someone being bullied at school, I took it personally, and instead of minding my own business, I would run to defend them. Thus began my justifiable—and frequent—visits to the principal's office.

Andrea Edwards

Trouble at Home

Mom and Dad never again fought with each other, as they had back in Chile. Dad never hit mom again. However, the yelling and screaming never ceased. Life at home was emotionally draining. I felt a constant obligation to please everyone when I felt the friction of a fight coming on. I would try effortlessly to make my family laugh by putting on a clown show. I would jump up and down, make funny faces and sounds, all the while feeling as if I was ready to collapse emotionally. I had to constantly watch myself around my one sister, who had been affected greatly by the constants madness we grew up with. Simply the sight of my presence would set her off in a violent rage against me. She would attack me to the point of drawing blood. When I would demand justice be done, my parents did nothing, and Mom's words were always the same. She would say that I had to learn to understand my sister's anger toward me because she had witnessed Dad beating on Mom throughout the years and was traumatized by it. I would cry out, "We all witnessed the fights." Ignoring my plea, Mom would continue speaking in a condescending way. "And because you're so much like your father—cold, cruel, with no feelings, no emotions, no heart for anyone, always telling lies—you are a constant reminder to your sister of your father!" Mom's words cut deeply, leaving me hurt, confused, and carrying the guilt of my sister's anger. At this point, I promised Mom that I would forgive my sister whenever she hit me, and learn to understand her, and love her. I honestly vowed in my heart to do so.

My sister's rage against me continued, and at Mom's command, I began locking myself in my room. But that didn't always keep me safe.

Mom and Dad warned me not to say a word about what was going on at home to anyone, and if I ever did, I would never be allowed to go to church again. Their threats terrified me, as I loved spending time with my church family. I promised my parents, that I would never say a word to anyone.

The Letter

I could have never imagined what was about to take place at school. The worst nightmare anyone could possibly go through was about to erupt, and I was at the center of it all.

An immigrant girl from Haiti who had been in Canada longer than I had and who could speak English well enough, began finding letters in her locker every morning, stating that someone was watching her. This went on for weeks and, through the intercom, the entire school was cautioned about the letters and warned that whoever it was had better stop. However, the letters continued and even got worse, threatening her with death.

The poor girl became fearful. She was always crying and looking over her shoulder. Some of the students began keeping her company at all times.

One day while I was in class, I was called to the office. When I arrived, I saw there were other teachers present, including my gym teacher who was also my homeroom teacher. I was interrogated by the principal about whether I knew who was sending the letters.

Confused, I answered, "No."

What the principal said next shocked me.

"We suspect you are the one writing the letters!"

Alarmed, I said, "No! It's not me!"

They didn't believe me, and they made sure that I understood that I was their suspect. I left the office crying at the awful accusation, and noticed that I was being watched. I went to the washroom and splashed water on my face while I cried.

I went back to class feeling nervous and sick to my stomach, feelings that would stay with me for weeks and months to come.

I found out some time later that the letters were being put together with cut-out letters from magazines that were glued to paper and put into the girl's locker. When she would open her locker in the morning, she would find them and begin screaming and crying, which got everyone's attention. I began to resent her, because every time she found a letter, I was the one being accused falsely.

I couldn't understand how the teachers could suspect me, when I was new to the country. I could hardly speak, read, or write the English language, and my homeroom teacher knew I was almost always a few minutes late due to our three-bus route to school.

Weeks passed and, to my shocking horror, word got out to the entire school that I was the main suspect.

Every day, I felt like I was living in a nightmare from hell. In class, I was ignored by the teachers and bullied by some of the students. Some started physical altercations with me. My homeroom teacher, who had been kind to me once, would now participate with all her students and completely ignore me. When attendance was called, my name was not mentioned. In gym, I was made to sit on the bench for the whole class while everyone else participated. When I would put my hand up for help with my studies, I was purposely ignored, and given dirty looks by some of the teachers. Nevertheless, desiring to move forward and wanting to understand what was being taught (though afraid of rejection), I still managed to get the courage to go and get help from the teachers, always giving them the benefit of the doubt. But when I did, I was brushed away by short, cutting words and accusatory looks. I would walk back to my desk feeling the painful waves of rejection in my heart.

I began to dread going to school, so I began skipping classes, wandering the streets alone until school was over. Then I would go back to meet up with my younger sister who attended the same school, and we would go home together.

The Dress

In my home economics class, we started a project making an item of clothing of our choosing, each of us having to buy our own pattern. I felt sick at the thought of asking Mom for money for this, and to have her say no.

After a struggle to convince Mom that I needed to buy a pattern and material for my class project, she finally agreed to the cheapest one we could find: a shapeless dress pattern. That was fine with me, as I would have a new dress to wear to church. I felt a sense of happiness for a change and couldn't wait to get started. The excitement helped to take my mind a little bit off the nightmare I was living in.

When I opened the pattern, to my surprise, there were lines, numbers and words I couldn't make out. However, I wasn't the only one who couldn't understand; most of the class had their hands up for help. Fearing rejection, I patiently waited for the teacher to finish helping all the other students, and when everyone was busy with their heads down concentrating on their patterns, I nervously put my hand up for help. When the teacher finally approached me, she looked disappointed and angry.

With my limited English, I nervously asked her to help me with the pattern. Her expression and words—at least the ones I was able to understand—stabbed me like a knife. "You and I both know that you have no problem reading those instructions all by yourself!" she said, and walked away.

I had hoped no one would notice her cruel words, facial expression, and evil tone, but everyone did because she had spoken loudly. All eyes fell on me. I wanted to run out of the class and hide, never to return again.

Through my watery eyes, I stared at my pattern with the foreign words and lines, and suddenly a willful determination came upon me, and I made up my mind, that somehow, I was going to get that dress done, with or without the teacher's help.

In my mind, I flashed back to Santiago when I would watch my Abuelita making us dresses, which she did often, as dresses were all we wore through the summer months. She would cut the material to her paper patterns according to their shape on the large dining room table, and I remember her clearly saying to me one day as I watched her work, "You always have to cut a few sizes bigger than the size you want it to be."

That's what I was going to do. So while the teacher went around helping everyone in class, I began working on my pattern, and every time the teacher would walk past me, she'd shake her head at me in a condemning, accusatory way.

The weeks went by and, though I took longer than everybody else, I finally finished my dress by myself. I couldn't wait to take it home and try it on and wear it to church.

When I got home, I ran upstairs to my bedroom in excitement to try it on. But to my disappointment, it turned out to be double, even triple, my size. I was practically swimming in it. I threw myself on the bed and cried.

The persecution was overwhelming, so I continued skipping school. When I got home, my parents had already been informed of my absence. They refused to listen to or believe anything I tried to tell them in regards to what was happening at school. So I continued being punished and sent to my room.

Andrea Edwards

My Friends

I got used to spending hours alone in my bedroom, which consisted of your basic four walls, all bare, my bed, a night table, a dresser with most drawer's empty, and a flimsy metal shelf that would tip over at the slightest touch. My closet was a fair size, but practically empty, with no more than a handful of items hanging to one side. The foot of my bed was decorated with used stuffed animals I had picked up at the Manpower office for free. I didn't care that they were used; I was just happy to have them, as I had never owned stuffed animals before, and the more I spent time alone in my room, the more they became my friends.

One was a clown with tears on his face that reminded me of myself as I kept a smile on the outside, but was crying on the inside much of the time.

I sketched and colored my stuffed animals, and was surprised to see how accurate my drawings were to what they actually looked like. Feeling proud of myself at finding perhaps an untapped talent that Mom and Dad might also be proud of, I jumped from my bed and excitedly ran downstairs to show off my drawing accomplishments, hoping and longing for some recognition. Mom looked at it, gave them a quick smile, and said, "Child's drawings" I went back to my room feeling like a worthless child.

Nothing I did was good enough for anyone it seemed.

At night before falling asleep, I made each of my stuffed animal's beds on the floor beside my bed, using my clothes. I would tuck them in and give them all goodnight kisses. Showing them love, and telling them that I loved them before going to sleep was important to me. Something I was desperately longing for inside: someone to hold me and to kiss me goodnight, assuring me that all would be well.

Andrea Edwards

Attacked

One day in a portable classroom at school when class was almost over, I waited to get help from the teacher about homework she was assigning. I was the last in line on purpose, just in case she rejected me. I didn't want to be humiliated in front of everyone. When my turn finally came, and I began speaking, the teacher quickly took her eyes of me, grabbed her things from her desk and rushed out the door, stating she didn't have any time. Feeling the stabbing pain of rejection, I walked away slowly, as tear filled my eyes. I wanted to understand and learn so badly so I could focus on my studies and move ahead. But how was I supposed to when no one wanted to help me?

With my head hung low, I was slowly moving toward the door when, suddenly, a boy bigger than most grown men came from behind and attacked me. It was the brother of the girl who had been receiving the letters. He picked my one-hundred-pound body up from the floor and pinned me against the wall. I tried to push him away, but with all his weight on me, I couldn't move. He then began fondling my breast forcefully and tried to force his hand down my pants with his body weight on me. Not able to move, I panicked and began screaming for him to leave me alone. Somewhat frightened of my screams, he looked behind him toward the door. That made him lose his tight grip on me, and I was able to free myself and run out of the portable classroom into the school. Angry that I had gotten away from him, he yelled out the door,

"I am going to get you!"

After the attack, I was always watching my back, scared that he would follow me and try to hurt me again. I knew I had no one to turn to for help. I was on my own, and I was so afraid.

My younger sister knew about the persecution I was going through. She suggested that I go and speak to the home economics teacher because she was nice to her, and my sister believed the teacher would be nice to me, too, and help stop the persecution against me. I told my sister that it was not a good idea. I didn't mention that this was the teacher who had been unwilling to help me with my dress project. However, my sister insisted that I speak with her and, to put her at ease, I agreed.

After school one day, we walked to the teacher's classroom. When we got there, I stood outside, frozen with fear and unable to enter. My sister went in to tell the teacher that I wanted to speak with her. The teacher came out and stood in front of me, staring at me with a cold look on her face, not saying a word, just waiting for me to speak.

The second I saw her cold expression, my fears were confirmed. I knew she wasn't going to help me. I wanted to walk away right there and then. Nevertheless, beside me stood my sister, pleading with me to declare my innocence to her. With my limited English, I said,

"I didn't write the letters. Please believe me."

With the same cold, calculated expression she already wore, she responded with a sharp tone.

"I don't believe you!" She repeated herself over and over again. The pain I felt in my heart was unbearable. I ran out of the school, crying.

Andrea Edwards

Polygraph Test

Shortly after, while in class, I was called to the principal's office. To my surprise, when I arrived, my sister was already there and had been interrogated regarding me. Also present were two police officers waiting to take both my sister and me away to be interrogated using a polygraph test, to see if we were telling the truth or not. The presence of the police in uniforms terrified me, bringing back memories of the military back home in Santiago.

The police ushered me and my sister to the back seat of the police car, and took us to the police station. I was afraid, but I hid my feelings to be strong for my sister who was crying with fear. I told her everything was going to be fine, and that they'd soon bring us back to school. I didn't know if that was true. I just didn't want my sister to be afraid.

When we arrived at the building, I was ushered into a room and hooked up to some wires. I remember asking the man who was attaching me to the wires, if it hurt. When they were finished with us, we were taken back to school.

My parents were called and informed about the letters and my involvement in them. But instead of coming to my defense, they jumped on board with my accusers, and the trouble at home escalated.

The results of the polygraph test came back, but I was never told what they were. I was just called down to the office and informed that I was being expelled from school. I was ordered to gather all my things from my locker, and to leave the school premises immediately because I wasn't welcome there any longer. Once again, the pain of rejection was too much to bear. I walked toward my locker, crying hard, this time not caring who saw me. All I could feel was the overwhelming pain in my heart.

After my dismissal, the letters continued coming. Now detectives were busy trying to find out who the real culprit was, because the poor girl was living in so much fear.

A short while later, their work paid off and they found the real culprit. To everyone's shock and disbelief, the culprit turned out to be the girl herself. That's right. She was writing the letters to herself. The teachers and the entire school were in shock.

The girl's brother, who had attacked me in the portable classroom, mentioned to my sister that his sister was sent to get psychiatric help, and that he thought she had turned crazy since their uncle, who was a witch doctor, had arrived from Haiti and moved in with them.

I didn't learn until much later that the school had telephoned my parents to let them know of the outcome, and to say that, if I so desired, I could come back.

It was a new beginning for me. Spring was in the air, and I had just turned fourteen. Soon September would arrive, and I would be starting fresh in a new school. I hoped my life would take a turn for the better, and all would go well.

I promised myself that I was going to do well and excel in school and eventually become the professional Mom wanted me to become, and make her proud of me.

But unbeknownst to me, things were not going to go that way. Life was about to get darker than it had ever been.

Chapter Four
Help Me!

Church had pretty much become the only place I looked forward to. I didn't feel safe anywhere else. As a youth group, we did so many things together: we went skating, played soccer, and met in each other's homes for bible study and prayer on a weekly basis. As a choir, we visited English-speaking churches and sang for them in Spanish. But all of it was about to come to an end for me.

Our church had welcomed a man named Cain. He was in his late twenties, and apparently related to a very well-known musician from Chile. People in the church quickly became fond of him because of his family history and musical talents. He could play the guitar well and sing beautifully. He quickly took over the youth choir.

Within a short period, Cain began dating my good friend, Martha, who was the same age as me, barely fourteen. There was talk in the church of their considerable age difference. However, to everyone's knowledge, she had her parents' consent and blessing and, because of his status, the matter was quickly put to rest.

As time passed, Cain started hanging around us young girls more than ever because of his relationship with Martha.

There was something about him I didn't like or trust, as his behavior would take me by surprise, sometimes. For instance, one time I was coming out of the washroom which was located in the church basement, and no one was around. On my way up the stairs, Cain appeared out of nowhere and ran up behind me, startling me, and then quickly pulled me toward him to give me a kiss, calling it a "Christian kiss." Right after, he continued running up the stairs innocently as if he had done no wrong. But to me, it didn't seem like an innocent kiss, but a guilty one. Nevertheless, I naively disregarded his possible motive because, after all, he was courting my good friend, Martha.

Violation

Early on a Monday morning in the spring of 1979, only a few weeks after I had been expelled from school, the phone rang. It was Cain wanting to know if I could accompany him to a doctor's appointment as a translator. I told him that I would have to ask my mom's permission, and that she was at work. He insisted that he couldn't wait and that he desperately needed my help right away. I agreed, nervously, as my English was poor and I wondered what help I would really be. I asked if my younger sister could come along as well but, in an apologetic tone, Cain said,

"No. She can't come because the back seat of my car is full of stuff and I don't have the time to clean it up and I need to go now!"

Since he only lived a few blocks away from us, he was waiting outside my front door beeping his horn within minutes. The doctor's appointment turned out to be a dental appointment to get his teeth cleaned, and he didn't need my help at all.

On his way to drop me off, he said that he had to make a quick stop at his house and asked me to come in and wait. In the kitchen, he offered me some juice and, while he guzzled his drink back, he suddenly looked concerned and said,

"I promised my sister that I would clean the bedrooms upstairs, and she is due home any minute now. Can you help me clean up?"

Not looking forward to it, I agreed.

He showed me his bedroom, and asked me to clean it while he cleaned his sister's room. Everything looked pretty tidy, except for his bed, so I began making his bed when, suddenly, Cain came from behind and pushed me onto it. He threw himself on top of me and forcefully began rubbing his already exposed body against mine. Startled and confused, I told him to stop, and expected him to. But he didn't. He only became more forceful. I yelled for him to stop, but he would not listen. Instead, he forcefully pulled my clothes off and raped me.

Crying, I closed my eyes tightly, desperately waiting for him to end his evil deed.

When it was over, he got up calmly and began getting dressed as if he had done nothing wrong. He then told me to go wash myself immediately.

Feeling panicked, I headed for the washroom. My body was shaking so much that I thought I would fall. I washed myself in the tub, and noticed fluids. Disgusted, I washed it all away quickly. When I was finished, with my clothes practically hanging off me, I slammed the washroom door open, hurried down the stairs, and ran out the door, into the direction of my home.

All the while, I felt like I was ready to faint and collapse to the ground, but the will to get away from him gave me the strength to keep running. When I got home, I ran upstairs to the washroom, turned the hot shower on, and got under the hot water. My body was still violently trembling. I washed and scrubbed hard, trying to wash away the horrible feelings. I noticed some bruising up and down my arms and legs from being held down, and the more I looked at my body, the more the sight of my nakedness made me feel fearful, vulnerable, and ashamed. I got out of the shower and got dressed quickly. I put on layers and layers of clothes, trying to cover up as much of my body as possible. I then went and sat inside my closet, hugging my knees tightly, rocking back and forth, and weeping uncontrollably, hoping the horrible feelings would just go away.

Mom and Dad got home and resumed their day as usual. It had become customary for me to eat quickly and leave the
table to avoid confrontations with the other sister before they all sat down to eat as a family. However, when supper was ready and I heard Mom yelling for me to come down and eat, I had no appetite and I didn't want to be around anyone. But Mom demanded that I come downstairs to eat.

By the time I did, everyone was already sitting down, eating. I sat, looking down toward my plate, trying to behave as normally as possible, so that no one would suspect anything. But I dropped my fork, and the noise of it hitting the floor scared me so much that, without warning, I broke out crying, hard.

"What's wrong with you!?" Mom asked, sternly.

"I am not feeling well. May I be excused, please?"

I was excused.

My parents didn't concern themselves with me, probably because they were used to seeing me upset, mostly because of the fights between me and my sister, and also because it was Monday, which meant choir practice, and they knew I wouldn't miss church for the world.

The hours passed and then I heard Mom yelling from downstairs that Dad was waiting to drive me to church.

I panicked and pleaded with her to let me stay home. But Mom wouldn't take no for an answer, and demanded that I go. The drive to church felt like I was reliving the nightmare. Dad quickly dropped me off, leaving me in the parking lot of the church, alone.

I walked slowly toward the sanctuary where choir practice took place. When I got to the doorway, I stood frozen, looking in. I noticed that most of the leaders and youth were gathered up front, socializing, as they always did before practice began. Cain was conversing with one of the youth leaders. When he turned my way, his eyes met mine. His face divulged fear, and guilt!

His eyes seemed to say,

"Are you angry? Are you going to say anything? Or are you going to pretend like nothing happened?"

But then he turned around and continued chatting and laughing as if he had done no wrong. At that moment, I felt intense hatred toward him. Just looking at him disgusted me.

Again, he glanced at me and this time he actually gave me a smile, as if being friendly would make the wrong he had done right. No, it would not! Just the sight of him made me feel as if the rape was happening all over again, and I just couldn't stand it!

I had to get out of there, fast. But where was I to go? Who would help me?

Just then I saw Elsa, a lady from the choir in her late twenties whom I had begun to call Aunt Elsa.

She was sitting at the very back pew.

Instantly, I threw myself under the pews and frantically began to slide under each one, all the way to her feet. When I finally got to her, the pain in my heart opened up like a dam, and the tears came flooding out, as I cried for help.

Alarmed, Elsa grabbed my hand and took me to the washroom.

I told her about the rape, holding back the gruesome details. I begged her not to say a word to my parents because they would only blame me and not help me like she thought they would.

Elsa knew nothing of my life at home. She held my parents in high esteem and encouraged me to speak to them.

I was afraid. I couldn't even get through half a sentence without them declaring me guilty; my life at home was bad enough already. Adding the rape would make it a thousand times worse. I couldn't imagine it; surely, I would die.

Elsa and I never stayed for choir practice. We left and went to her house, where I spent the night.

At home, I spent all day in my room, silently weeping throughout the day and night.

Days later, my parents found out what happened through Elsa. Dad took me for a drive in the car and began asking me questions about the rape, wanting details. I didn't feel comfortable speaking to Dad, nor did I trust that he had my best interests at heart, so I quickly gave him a short version of the rape. Dad pounded his fist on the steering wheel and drove back home saying nothing.

My parents called the pastor immediately. When the pastor learned what had happened to me, he advised us on how we were to respond by quoting a scripture from the bible found in the book of Daniel, Chapter 6.

"My God sent his angel and he shut the mouths of the lions."

The pastor interpreted this scripture as meaning we must say nothing about the rape.

I sat on the stairs listening to their back-and-forth discussion, and their final decision to do nothing. I felt angry inside. I wanted justice to be served against the rapist. I wanted him punished! But according to the pastor, and apparently according to God, the right decision was to say nothing, to keep the rape quiet in order to keep the peace in the church.

What about my peace? I sure didn't have any since the rape. I felt so hurt and angry that I ran to my room and threw myself on the bed and cried hard.

I didn't understand it then, but the decision the pastor made was not God's decision, but man's choice to manipulate God's Word, empowered by the fear of men, rather than the fear of God.

We continued attending church as if nothing had happened. I sat with Elsa, away from the youth, while lies, gossip, and innuendos about me spread like wildfire. In many people's eyes, I was the guilty one.

The rapist, on the other hand, appeared to be esteemed in reverence, as if he had done no wrong.

As such, going to church became a punishment that I refused to bear, so I stopped. My family continued to go for a little while longer, but they also eventually stopped attending church, as well.

At home, I was made to feel as if the rape was my fault. I was constantly blamed for having brought so much shame to the family.

Since the rape, my relationship with my sister went from bad to worse. I had to constantly stay clear from her violent attacks toward me. I had nowhere to turn to for help. I felt so alone. The pain in my heart became too heavy to bear. I just wanted one thing, the very thing I had feared so many times throughout my childhood: death. I wanted to die!

I grabbed a bottle of pills that I had found in the washroom medicine cabinet, and swallowed them all. My parents found the empty bottle and took me to the emergency room. I never came home that night. I was hospitalized for months.

Hospital

I began seeing a psychiatrist, and she wanted to know everything about me, focusing on my upbringing and my relationship with my parents and siblings. I spoke highly of my family, but I guess too highly, because she saw right through me, somehow knowing I wasn't telling the truth. She told me that she wanted me to answer her questions truthfully and sincerely, and promised me that whatever I shared with her would stay between us.

In my limited English, and thanks to her immense patience and will to understand me, I began sharing some information about my life at home.

She put an immediate stop to my family visiting me altogether.

In one of our sessions, she made a statement that surprised me, and whose full meaning I wouldn't appreciate until many years later. She said,

"Andrea, I have three daughters myself, and I would never, ever treat any of them the way you have been treated. Do you understand what I mean when I say that?"

I didn't understand it, because I didn't know any other life than the one in which I was brought up.

In another of our sessions, I told her about the fights with my sister, and her advice completely shocked me, as it was quite the opposite of what I had been taught. She said,

"The next time your sister hits you, I want you to hit her back—hard! I don't want you to put up with her abuse any longer! Do you understand?"

I couldn't believe her advice, especially coming from a doctor. I liked the fact that she was sticking up for me. However, her advice completely contradicted what I was told to do at home. I never got to share my stories about the school bullying, or the devastating rape; the subjects never came up. The doctor zeroed in on my family, and that was bad enough, she thought.

When I was discharged from the hospital, I was afraid to leave. I had experienced a sense of safety and care there that I had never known before, and had grown to love the psychiatrist and the hospital staff for showing me such kindness and love. I was encouraged to go and live with a foster family, but I was afraid and, rejected the offer.

My parents were called in a few weeks prior to my discharge, and we were counseled together by the psychiatrist. She spoke highly of me, and told them to treat me well because I was the type of daughter that many parents only wished they had, including her.

Upon hearing her kind words, my heart warmed and I wished that, if anyone would take me in, it would be her.

As she spoke, I glanced at my parents' faces. They looked void of any sincere emotions, and I knew the psychiatrist's words meant nothing to them.

Victoria Composite High

After the long and difficult spring and summer of 1979, September arrived, and I was starting fresh in high school.

I promised myself that I would try my best in my new school, learn the English language, and eventually graduate and go to university and make my parents proud of me.

Victoria Composite High School was also located in the downtown area, so the three-bus route continued. I made sure to wake up extra early so I wouldn't be late. I was enrolled in a split grade nine/ten class since I hadn't completed grade nine in my previous school.

Nervously, I walked from class to class, noticing once again that my clothes were going to be an issue by some of the looks some of the girls were giving me. This time, I knew better than to ask my parents for money, or take any. I had acquired a few pairs of jeans from the Manpower office we visited once in a while, and though they were second-hand and out of style, I used Mom's sewing machine to style them up-to-date. To my amazement, they fit perfectly on my slim frame.

In class, I listened attentively, trying hard to comprehend what was being taught and discussed so I wouldn't have to bother the teachers for their assistance. But once again I was having trouble understanding the English. Feeling nervous and anxious, I gathered the courage to go to the front and quietly ask the teacher for help. When he responded, he spoke loudly enough for the whole class to hear, and ended his sentence with a question for me.

"Do you understand now?" he asked, and followed it with a look, as if to say, "It's pretty self-explanatory. You would have to be really *stupid* not to understand!"

I turned to face the class and, to my horror, every eye in the room was staring right at me, as if they were waiting for my response. The scary thing was that I had hardly understood a word the teacher had said. Feeling panicked that everyone—including the teacher—would think I was stupid for not knowing the English language, I quickly said,

"Thank you," and walked back to my desk, with my head hung low.

As the weeks passed, I got nowhere, no matter how hard I tried to understand or how many times I gathered the courage to get up and ask for help. I began feeling panicked in the classrooms, knowing that it was only a matter of time before the teachers addressed me. I needed to find a way out of the nightmare I was in. But the nightmare was about to get worse.

In one of my classes, I noticed a girl who sat at the front of the class. She was quiet, reminding me much of myself. I wondered why she sat at the front to begin with, because every time there were class discussions, she would never speak. If she was as shy and frightened as I was, why was she sitting up in the front row?

After class. I followed her to the washroom and introduced myself. Her name was Karen.

I wasted no time and asked her straight out,

"Would you like to be my friend?"

She said, "Sure."

I was desperate for a friend, a friend who would stick with me through thick and thin, even if the whole school turned against me, as they had once. So I asked Karen again, "Would you like to be my *best* friend?"

Looking surprised, she smiled, and said, "Sure!"

Karen was from Nova Scotia and she, too, had just recently moved to Edmonton, so right from the start we had something in common. We were both new to the city, and new to the school.

We became inseparable. She did all the talking, and I did all the listening. When I did try to speak, she would laugh at my accent and teach me the correct pronunciation.

Karen had a deep voice with a Nova Scotia accent, and I had a quiet voice, but when I spoke English I'd pronounce the words just like her, even imitating her deep accent, which made her laugh.

Walking through the hallways of school one day, I was surprised to see Martha, Cain's girlfriend, attending the same school, as were some of her siblings. When I passed her in the hallway, I said hi, hoping we could be friends again. Before the rape, Martha was someone I had considered a true friend. But she ignored me on purpose, because she believed the lies from her rapist boyfriend.

Sometimes, I would see her with a group of girls and, as they walked by me, they would whisper to each other, and some of them would give me dirty looks.

One day, I was in a restaurant across from the school with Karen when Martha came in with a group of girls. On my way out, our eyes connected, so I said hello, hoping she would say hello back. But she didn't respond.

Feeling her betrayal, I retaliated and swore at her, not caring who heard me.

The weeks went by and, one day while in class, my name was paged through the intercom. When Howard, a popular, good-looking boy in the class heard my name paged, he jokingly said that I must have won a prize for being the most beautiful girl in the school.

He didn't keep quiet about his attraction to me. Everyone in class knew it. I couldn't wrap my head around it and thought: what could he possibly like, in me? So I ignored him as much as possible.

I walked the long hallways to the office, somewhat excited about the possibility of actually winning something. I had never won anything before. Then reality hit, and fear struck me. I had taken the journey to the principal's office way too many times before, and it had always been bad news.

I tried to rationalize my fear by telling myself that, all that was behind me.

I entered the office, gave the secretary my name, and was told to sit and wait; the principal would soon see me. I waited, never expecting what he was about to say.

When he approached me, he looked serious, and asked me straight out if I had been smoking in school.

Shocked, I answered,

"No! I don't smoke."

He didn't believe me, and said that people had seen me. He gave me a warning, and sent me back to class. I left the office feeling the weight of the accusation.

A few weeks went by before I was called to the office again. When I arrived, I was met by the principal and immediately warned of the consequences for smoking on school premises.

Alarmed, I said, "I don't smoke! Please believe me!"

But he wouldn't believe me. He said,

"Look, I wasn't born yesterday!" (His words, "Look I wasn't born yesterday!" were registered in my head.)

He continued: "Next time, you will be suspended from school!"

I left the office feeling the effects of the emotional roller coaster I was entering once again. Unable to control my tears, I rushed to the washroom and began splashing water on my face while I cried. The nightmare I so feared was back!

I returned to class and walked straight to my desk, which was at the very back, and sat with my head hung low, hoping no one would pay any attention to me or ask me any questions. However, Howard, who sat close to me, wanted to know why I was being called to the office again.

I said jokingly, "I won a prize."

He laughed, and nothing else was said.

The days and weeks passed, and I lived in constant fear and anxiety that I would be made a public spectacle in front of the whole school again, and that my only friends would desert me. I knew I couldn't survive alone. The pain in me was too great.

Howard began hanging out with Karen and me, and soon he began proudly introducing me to his friends as his Spanish girlfriend from San Diego, instead of Santiago.

I corrected his pronunciation a few times, but he didn't seem to get it and I giggled each time he said it. He also told everyone that I was going to be the most beautiful model in the world.

His admiration and fondness for me was something I didn't understand, and every time he made it known, I felt as if he was talking about someone else; not me. Nevertheless, being around him helped to numb some of the sad realities of my life.

One day, a group of us was sitting by the stairs near the school pool eating our lunch, and some of my friends were smoking. Suddenly, we were aggressively interrupted by the principal, along with two other male teachers. Those who were smoking quickly ran outside, and I, along with Karen and Howard, was left behind. The principal ordered Karen and Howard to leave the area, and I was taken back to the office with them.

Once in the office, the principal grabbed and pulled my ID which hung on my jacket, and said,

"You won't need this anymore! As of right now, you are expelled for smoking on school premises!"

He mentioned that my parents had been notified, which meant more trouble when I got home. I was then ordered to gather all my things from my locker and leave the school premises immediately.

I walked away, speechless at the false accusations. I felt numb from everything but the pains of rejection, which were back with a vengeance.

When I stepped out of the office, I noticed Martha standing with her girlfriends a distance away, looking at me and laughing, as if somehow they knew what had just happened. But that was impossible, I thought. There was no way she knew anything.

I focused on getting to my locker quickly, and gathered my things before any of my friends saw me and found out what had happened.

When I finished, I went to wait for the bus, not realizing that I was actually being followed.

I was standing shivering in the cold Edmonton winter, dreading my arrival at home and the chaos I knew awaited me there, when I was suddenly startled from my thoughts by someone yelling,

"Andrea!"

I looked back at the school, and there was a large group of girls heading toward me. There were approximately ten girls and I didn't recognize any of them. When they got close to me, they surrounded me in a circle, and one of them, began accusing me of gossiping about her. Then another girl accused me. And then another one.

With my limited English, I tried to explain that I didn't even know who they were. But it didn't matter what I said—their minds were made up. Someone had obviously fabricated lies to them about me. But *who*, I wondered.

Suddenly I began being attacked from every direction. They threw me over a two-foot wrought iron fence. My feet were dangling upward and my body landed on the snowy ground. The girls came at me, kicking me, punching me, pulling my hair, scratching me. I begged them to stop, but they viciously continued. I closed my eyes in agony, desperately hoping they would stop. At one point, as I was buried underneath all the bodies, I opened my eyes and got a glimpse of the pale blue sky above me and cried out to God for help.

Within seconds, I heard a man's voice, shouting with authority: "HEY, STOP!"

It was Howard and his buddies, coming to my rescue. When they got to me, they pulled the girls off of me, who then ran away. Howard picked me up, embracing me in his arms. My clothes were torn and bloody, and I could taste blood in my mouth.

Howard's concern for me was genuine. He wanted to take me back into the school to get medical help, but I refused, not wanting him to find out that I had been expelled and wasn't welcome in the school. As he held me close to him, he said, "It's a miracle we showed up when we did. They could have killed you!"

Was it a miracle? I wondered, because death sounded pretty good.

Howard insisted on taking me home, but I knew that would only make matters worse. When the bus arrived, I quickly thanked him for his help, said my goodbyes, and boarded the bus—alone. That was the last time I would see Howard.

Andrea Edwards

Please love me

I walked to the very back of the bus and sat down, feeling completely broken and rejected. My body was shaking from the beating. I glanced at my clothes, which were torn and bloody, and made an effortless try to hide some of the obvious damage—but there was no fixing the broken.

A middle-aged woman who was sitting across from me wouldn't take her eyes off of me, and her stare was as cold as the winter snow outside. For a moment, I wished I could see some warmth in her eyes, a sympathetic look so that I could open up and pour my broken heart to her while she held me in her arms, as a good mother would.

If only someone would just love me, I thought. That's all I wanted: just to be loved.

I exited the last bus to my home, dreading it, but, instead of going home right away, I wandered the cold streets for a few hours, until I couldn't stand the cold any longer.

By the time I approached the house, it had gotten dark.

I stood by the door, trying to gain the courage to knock.

I was so scared that I could feel my heart beating fast, and my stomach knotted in pain. I knew that as soon as I walked in the doors, all hell would break loose.

When I finally got the courage to knock, Mom and Dad came to the door and . . . all hell broke loose!

I desperately tried declaring my innocence, but my parents hit me, refusing to listen or believe anything I had to say. At one point, my father punched me in the face with such force that it sent me flying toward the handle of the door, and the impact split my forehead open. Blood came gushing out and flowed down my face. Feeling overwhelmed, I began crying, screaming, kicking, and punching the walls around me, putting holes through them, hoping that all the madness in my life would just stop!

When my parents saw my state of insanity, they stopped hitting me, and I was ordered to go to my room. They told me they weren't finished with me yet.

I lay in bed curled up on my side, feeling mentally, emotionally, and physically drained. All I wanted was to die!

I stared at my bedroom window, trying to muster the courage to jump and fall to my death.

I sat up on my bed staring at the window intensely, and suddenly my father barged into my room, closed the door behind him, and began removing his belt. As he did, the zipper of his pants came undone, exposing some of his underwear.

With a sarcastic smile, he said,

"Drop your pants! I am going to teach you a lesson you will never forget!"

Shocked, disgusted, and horrified at what I thought smelled and looked like rape, I yelled back,

"I am fourteen years old, and there is no way in hell I will drop my pants!"

He forcefully demanded that I obey him.

I lost it, and began hitting and throwing everything in sight. Having reached a lunatic state, I stopped suddenly and looked at him and said,

"If you touch me, I will kill you, or I will jump out that window to my death!"

If he didn't leave the room at that very second, I was going to follow through with one of my threats. One of us was going to die!

And then the unexpected happened.

Dad stood frozen, looking back at me, speechless. His face turned pale, as if he had seen a ghost. And to my surprise, he turned around and left the room.

I threw myself on the bed that was now half on the floor, crying, feeling completely drained. I realized one thing at that moment: this was not my home!

First thing in the morning, after everyone was gone, I was running away.

Chapter Five
Homeless

"Even if a mother should forget her child, I will never forget you. I have written your name on the palms of my hands." Isaiah 49:15,16

Morning came, and I waited until everyone was gone from the house. Then I began packing my belongings. I managed to fit everything I needed into one garbage bag. At fourteen, I wasn't thinking about the facts of life—that I didn't have any money, or a place to go. I had my clothes and transit pass, and that was all I needed to get out of the hell I was in.

I got on the bus, dragging my garbage bag along, and sat at the very back. People stared at me as if they knew I was running away, but no one said a word. I was now officially homeless, in a country with a language I could hardly speak or understand, and with shattered dreams of ever being able to complete school.

I exited the final bus on Jasper Avenue, in downtown Edmonton. There were loads of people walking in every direction, so I joined the flow of the crowd, pretending to be on my way somewhere like everyone else. However, I stood out like a sore thumb dragging my garbage bag, which was a real burden to carry.

After hours of wandering the streets going nowhere, I got tired and began looking for a place to find shelter for the night. I walked into the entrance of the train station and sat on the garbage bag so it wasn't so noticeable, and pretended to look as if I was there with a purpose, waiting for someone, and not just a runaway kid with nowhere to go.

Night arrived, bringing the darkness with it. I continued sitting at the entrance of the train station where it was lit up, with strangers coming and going. Some of the men stared at me intensely, as if they were ready to approach me, and that made me feel afraid. As the traffic jam of people quieted down, the feelings of loneliness gripped me, and now they were entangled by the fear of strange men lurking around me. I nestled my face in my coat as the unwelcomed tears began to flow, and eventually fell asleep.

Morning came quickly, and the days began to roll by. During the days, I would wander the streets, stores, and malls for hours. Every time I walked passed a restaurant, the smell of food made my stomach growl wildly. I was so hungry, having had nothing to eat in days. Once in a while, I would find food in a garbage can, but people always seemed to be staring, so I would shy away from it. At nights, I would make it back to the entrance of the train station to fall asleep.

But the nights were becoming more fearful, with strange men staring at me and some even approaching me to ask if I had a place to go, before immediately inviting me to come with them. Their approach frightened me and encouraged me to find somewhere else to stay.

During the days, I boarded different buses and sat at the very back for hours as they took the same route over and over again, until the bus drivers would notice me and kick me out.

One day, I boarded a bus whose route took me close to my friend Karen's house. I exited immediately, and walked over to her house with my garbage bag. I briefly confided my situation to her, trusting her not to say a word to anyone. She grabbed the garbage bag and hid it out of sight from her mom, then pulled me into her house and rushed me to the basement. Later, she asked her mom if I could stay for a little while, and her mom agreed to a few days.

Karen took me to a social services office immediately. She said they would find me a place to live and give me money. I had never heard of such a place before. When I was called in, Karen came with me. She told the social worker about my predicament and needs, and the worker immediately asked me why I couldn't go back home to live with my parents. I froze, not wanting to say anything against my parents, but the worker insisted on knowing. She asked me questions about my relationship with my parents, but I sat nervously quiet, and didn't respond. Then all of a sudden, Karen burst out and said,

"They beat her up! Look!" She pointed at the cut on my forehead, and lifted up my shirt to show the social worker my bruises.

I pulled back abruptly from Karen and gave her a dirty look. I felt angry that she had betrayed me, as I had shared what happened at home in confidentiality. The social worker was now looking at me with shock on her face. She said,

"Do you know that your parents can go to jail for beating you?"

I knew what they did to people in jail back home.

I responded naively, in my parents' defense that not all the bruises were from them, but from a fight at school. The worker stood up from her chair sharply, stating that she would be right back, and left the office in a hurry. I sat there worried about my parents.

"She's gone to get you some help," Karen said, sounding excited. "They'll find you a place to live, and give you some money. You should be happy."

I wasn't happy. I was afraid, wondering what was going to happen to my parents. I asked Karen if my parents were going to jail. Her answer panicked me.

"I sure hope so! Your parents should learn not to beat on their kids. In this country, when parents beat on their kids, they go to jail!"

In a panic, I jumped out of the chair, and walked out of the office and out of the building, disappointed and horrified at how low I had fallen. Karen followed behind me, saying, "Where are you going? You can't leave now! These people are going to help you!"

I kept walking.

Karen tried to convince me to go back, because her mom would not let me stay at her house much longer.

"That's okay," I said. "I would rather live in the streets than have my parents put in jail."

Beer and Cigarettes

The weekend arrived, and Karen brought some beer to the basement. I had never tasted beer before and when I took a sip, I thought it tasted horrible. She also smoked cigarettes and offered me one. When I lit one up and took a drag, I began coughing uncontrollably. Karen laughed, and showed me the proper way to inhale. After a long while of gagging and coughing, I finally learned to inhale.

So there we were, the two of us, fourteen years old, in her parents' basement, drinking and smoking. After drinking a few beers, I tried getting up to go to the washroom, but instead, I fell to the floor. I was drunk. I could hear Karen laughing. She couldn't believe that I had gotten drunk on only a few beers. After a couple more, I tried to stand, but the room began spinning uncontrollably and I fell to the floor—hard.

Karen helped me to her bed in her room, which was in the basement, and I don't remember anything after that.

Sometime later, that same night I awoke to someone fondling me. I opened my eyes and there was a light on, giving the room a red-light effect. I could see a male figure sitting at the side of the bed, and realized it was Karen's sister's boyfriend. I panicked and tried pushing him away, but my hands missed him and the room began spinning uncontrollably. He came close to me, grabbed my hands gently, and whispered,

"It's okay, I won't hurt you. I just want to touch you; you're so beautiful."

Afraid and unable to fight back I lay there, defenseless, while he fondled and kissed my body. Then the door slammed open and his girlfriend barged into the room in shock and obvious disbelief at what she saw. She began yelling, and crying, hitting both me and him. He pulled her away from me and they both left the room.

In the shock of it all, I tried getting out of the bed, and fell hard on the floor. Karen came into the room and said, "Mom says you have to leave now!"

I began gathering my things, falling hard in every direction.
Karen's mom came down into the room and said, "I want her out, now!"
Karen said, "She's leaving! But she's in no condition to go right this minute; she can't even stand up straight!"

Even though I was intoxicated, Karen's words in my defense echoed in my ears. In my eyes, she was a true friend.

It was well past midnight when I left Karen's house. Karen came with me.

Central Edmonton was known for its party homes. After leaving Karen's house, we walked by a party taking place on the main floor of an apartment building. We walked right in and joined the crowd. People were spread out everywhere, drinking, doing drugs, some of them passed out. The apartment was unfurnished. Karen and I found a corner to sit in, and she jokingly said,

"Boy, there are a lot cute guys here. I wouldn't mind staying! But I have to get going, or else we're both going to be looking for a place to stay."

She left after a quick "See you around."

Alone and frightened, I curled up in a corner, watching my surroundings. Strangely, no one paid any attention to me. No one even looked my way, as if I wasn't even there. Eventually, I began to doze off, but I woke throughout the night to survey my surroundings before falling back asleep.

Then suddenly, I woke up to someone yelling, "Everybody out!"

It was daylight. I headed for the streets.

During the day, I walked everywhere, stopping at arcades and coffee shops to ask for a glass of water; sometimes, I would get a free cup of coffee. At night, I headed downtown and slept at the entrance of the subway station.

I no longer had my garbage bag with me; I had left it at Karen's. All I had was my duffel bag, with a change of clothes and some personal belongings.

As the weeks and months rolled by, I became familiar with some of the party houses in the area. I would discreetly walk in, pretending I was part of the crowd, find a washroom, wash up and then find a closet to hide away, and fall asleep for the night. In the mornings, I would head for the streets. I was always hungry, and the only source of food I had was people's leftover junk food.

Andrea Edwards

Someone, Please Love Me

One day, I decided to head to the south side of Edmonton, in search of a lady from the church for whom I had once babysat, hoping she would let me stay at her place for a while. I was almost sure that I remembered where she lived, but once I got there, all the houses looked the same. I knocked at the house that most resembled hers only to find out that it wasn't. After hours of going from house to house knocking, it began to get dark. Feeling panicked, I began rushing, knocking at every door in the hopes that, by some stroke of luck, the next person opening the door would be her. But there was a stranger's face behind every door, and before I knew it, it was dark. I realized that I was completely lost in the middle of a maze, where every home, every tree, and every street looked the same.

Feeling overwhelmed with fear and panic, I began walking down an unknown street hoping to find a bus shelter where at least I could wait for a bus to get me out of the hellish maze I was lost in. After walking for some time, I found a shelter, and waited for a bus. My bus pass had long ago expired, and I didn't have any money, so I hoped that the driver would be nice enough to give me a ride to the train station downtown, where at least I could find shelter from the cold.

After some time, a bus finally arrived, and when the driver opened the door, I told him straight away that I didn't have any money, and begged him for a free ride downtown. He closed the door in my face and drove off without uttering a word.

I wandered back into the shelter, and sat on the cold concrete floor, shivering from both the cold and the pain of rejection my heart knew too well. As the tears flowed down my face, I longed for someone to love me. *Just love me.* That's all I wanted.

Suddenly, I heard the noise of another bus coming to a stop. I heard the door open and someone exiting the bus. I made no attempt to move, afraid of being rejected again.

The bus driver yelled out to me, "I am the last bus driving by here tonight."

I asked him if he was going downtown.
"No." he answered. So I shook my head no.
The lady that had exited the bus overheard the conversation, and while she was getting ready to cross the street, she looked back at me and asked, "Don't you have anywhere to go? A place to sleep tonight?"
"No," I told her.
"If you'd like, you may sleep in my house for tonight, but you must leave early in the morning before my parents wake up, around five." I said, "Yes, please! Thank you!"

Her large condominium townhouse—from what I could see of it—was decorated beautifully. She asked me if I was hungry. I was starving; but I was afraid to say yes, and risk getting kicked out, so I said no, and my stomach protested loudly.

She showed me to the room upstairs where I could sleep, mentioning that it was the room of her sister, who was away at university. The room had a beautiful canopy bed, the kind most girls dream of having. On her way out the door she said,

"Remember, you have to leave by five o'clock in the morning."

I promised I would, and thanked her. I headed straight for the bed. When I sat on it, it squeaked so loudly that I nervously jumped up, afraid of waking her parents. I waited a few more seconds and gave it another try, but no matter how careful or quiet I was, the bed still squeaked loudly. I tried to ignore the noise and closed my eyes tightly and got under the covers. I lay motionless, in fear of being found out and getting kicked out.

It was a bright night, and the curtains in the room were wide open, so I could see the room fairly clear. I kept my eyes fixed on a wall clock that hung straight across from the bed to make sure I was up and out by five in the morning. As I lay in the beautiful room, I couldn't escape the feelings of loneliness and abandonment. The tears began to flow, and I whispered quietly, over and over again, "*Pleeeaase . . . someone love me.*"

Five o'clock came quickly and I had hardly slept a wink. The lady came into the room to wake me up, but I was already awake, and ready to go.

She accompanied me down the stairs and before leaving, I asked her if she was a Christian. She said no. I said,

"Thank you for letting me stay in your home, and God bless you!" I was felt so thankful to her, and at the same time I realized that Jesus still held a special place in my heart.

Andrea Edwards

The Call

I was tired of wandering the cold streets, having nowhere to sleep and no food to eat. Nights were always the worst.

The need to find shelter before the day was through weighed heavily upon me. I walked downtown, taking wrong turns here and there, but daylight was on my side, and before sundown, I found my way back to Jasper Avenue.

I decided I would call home, hoping things would be different.

I made the call from an arcade, across from the high school I used to attend. Mom answered, and as soon as she heard my voice, she began scolding me for having brought so much shame to the family.

Soon, I heard Dad in the background wanting to speak with me. He came to the phone and, in a friendly manner, asked how I was doing and where I was calling from. I told him my location, and as soon as he got the information he was looking for, his friendly tone turned to anger. Dad was unpredictable. One moment he could be the nicest person, and the next he could be mean and cruel. His personality shifts always took me by surprise.

As Dad continued talking, he said that if I wanted to come home, it would be according to their rules. Then he began stating them: I wouldn't be allowed to leave the house, I couldn't have any friends, there would be no phone use, and, most important of all, I would have to apologize to the whole family for all the trouble and shame I had caused everyone!

When Dad was finished with his demands, he insisted that I give him an answer that very moment. Hurt and confused, I hung up the phone.

Later on the same day, Dad appeared at the arcade. He ordered something to drink and gave me a sardonic smile from a distance, acting as if he didn't know me.
Eventually, he began talking to people in his broken English, while still ignoring me. Then he began playing pool, looking at me once in a while with the same smile. Finally, after a while, he approached me and whispered in my ear,
"Are you coming with me, or not!?"
I could tell that Dad wasn't sincere in his attempt to bring me home, and because I didn't trust or feel safe to be around him alone, I said,
"No."
"Fine." he answered with a sarcastic laugh, and left the arcade.

Years later, I found out from my younger sister that when Dad had gotten home that night, he had fabricated lies about me, announcing to everyone in the family that I was out there behaving worse than a prostitute, sleeping around with everyone. The truth was that even though I was living in the streets, I was still a virgin. The rape that had taken place almost a year ago was just that: rape!

Choice

One night as the arcade was closing, I was getting ready to leave and find somewhere to sleep for the night when one of the guys I played pool with approached me and said,

"I have been watching you. You don't have any place to go, do you?"

Feeling embarrassed, I said, "No."

"If you'd like, you can come and stay at my house for the night. It's not much, but I have a TV, a pool table, and a sofa in the basement where you can sleep."

I said yes. Anywhere was better than the cold streets.

When we arrived at his house, his basement looked like your typical unfinished basement: dark, gray, and with a cold, damp feel to it. I was a little nervous, not sure what to expect from him, though he seemed nice enough. But now that we were alone, would he change? I wondered.

He let me take a shower. I did, but kept my eyes glued to the door, making sure he didn't come in. Once done, we began playing pool, and suddenly, he approached me from behind. When I turned around, he was only a breath away from my face, and he began kissing me.

I froze in fear, not knowing what to do. I was in his house, and if I tried to stop him, would he throw me out to the dark, cold streets?

What happened next surprised me.

While he kissed me; he noticed that I wasn't responding, and said,

"We don't have to do this if you don't want to."

Surprised that he was asking me, giving me a choice, I nervously said,
"I don't want to."
He backed away slowly and said,
"That's fine. Let's play pool."

Instantly, this stranger, whom I only knew from hanging out in the arcade, had grown ten feet tall in my eyes. He had given me a choice, something I had never been given before, and it made me feel like I mattered. From that moment on, I felt comfortable being myself around him.

I would never forget his integrity and respect toward me.

David Chris

I continued hanging out in coffee shops and arcades during the day, and walking around looking for party homes at night. But I didn't always find one, and I didn't always end up at the train station, either. Some nights, I ended up hiding, huddled behind some building or back in an alley in someone's garage, hardly getting a wink of sleep because of both the cold and the fear of being found out, waiting anxiously for daylight to appear.

At the arcade across from the school I used to attend, I met a man in his early twenties who was half native. His name was David, but some people called him Chris, which confused me. When he found out that I had no place to live, he offered me a room in his house, which was not far from the arcade. He shared the upstairs of an older house with a native girl named Bridgett. She was in her mid-twenties and going to school to become a social worker.

David took me wherever he went, and eventually he began calling me his girlfriend. He introduced me to some of his family members, including his grandma, who was staying at a seniors' home. I liked her. From what I could tell, she had a warm, pleasant, and funny sense of humor.

One night while David was holding me close, he said the words I longed to hear:
"I love you. And I want to marry you and spend the rest of my life with you!"

I remember feeling numb at his words, unable to connect emotionally, but yet at the same time accepting my lot in life: namely, that this man was going to be my husband. And we became intimately involved.

Late one night, someone began knocking loudly at the front door. Dave went to see who it was, and a woman barged in, followed by a few small children crying and tailing behind her. She yelled at Dave, and then ran up the stairs to where I was. When she saw me, she began hitting me and calling me names. Dave pulled her away from me, saying,
"It's not her fault! It's not her fault!"

Then he disappeared out of the house with her, and I was left alone and confused, trying to understand what had just happened. Just then, Bridgett, the lady David shared the house with, came into the living room where I was standing and said,
"That's his wife! You better leave now, and don't ever come back!"
Wife? Wife! David was married!?

I was shocked, and speechless at the horrible news I had just learned.

The pain of betrayal and rejection stabbed my heart! I quickly gathered my belongings, threw them into my duffle bag, and left for the streets.

Kill Yourself!

It was dark, well past midnight, and I could hardly see past the flood of tears storming out my eyes. I didn't know where I was going, and I didn't care. I just wanted to die! Why should I continue to live when no one loved me?

As I walked the dark streets, heading toward 118 Avenue, I heard a loud voice say,
"WHY DON'T YOU JUST KILL YOURSELF? NO ONE CARES FOR YOU ANYWAY!"

The voice made sense to me, and I responded, "YES! That's what I will do! I will kill myself!"

My steps turned to a run, and with a shattered heart, closing my eyes, I threw myself into the street, and I began crossing, fully expecting to get hit by an oncoming vehicle at any moment, and not caring. The pain would soon be over. Or so I thought.

Suddenly, I heard the sound of screeching tires and froze in the middle of the street, waiting to get hit. Seconds passed, but nothing happened. The screeching stopped and a moment later a man yelled out,
"What are you trying to do? Kill yourself? Don't you know that God doesn't want you to kill yourself?"
What!? This guy was mentioning God?

Startled, I looked back in his direction and there stood a man wearing a white suit beside a large, fancy car, looking very serious, almost angry, and mentioning God!

Feeling scared, I ran across the street to the sidewalk, and began walking in the opposite direction, waiting for him to drive past me at any moment. But the seconds passed, and I neither heard nor saw him.

I looked back to see what was taking him, but he was nowhere to be found. It was like he had just vanished without a trace or sound. Something told me that this man was sent by God—and was perhaps an angel, dressed in a white suit, driving a fancy car, with a tough no-nonsense type attitude—to put the right kind of fear in me. The fear of wanting off the streets. Well it worked quickly, as I immediately wanted off the streets.

Chapter Six
The Promise

Feeling panicked, I began running. I ran right inside a phone booth and made a collect call to Elsa, the lady from the Spanish church whom I had run to for help when I'd been raped the previous year. I dialed her number as if someone was guiding my hand, surprised that I was able to remember it in a heartbeat, when I had previously dialed it only a few times.

As the phone rang, I hoped that she wouldn't be angry for calling her so late and hang up on me.

Elsa, however, happened to be waiting for my call because of a dream God had given her.

Elsa's Dream
In her dream, Elsa saw a little baby lamb in the basement of the church with all the other people of the church. The little lamb would try to get close to the people, wanting to be loved, but the people hated her and rejected her because she had a few stains. The abuse against the little lamb went on for a while, and as Elsa was watching it happen, she felt sad for her. So she picked her up in her

arms and tried showing the people that she was just an innocent, harmless baby lamb who simply wanted to be loved.

But the people didn't care. They continued to yell at the little lamb, hitting her and pushing her deeper down a set of stairs into a lower level of the basement.

The little lamb, scared and alone, desperately tried to get back up the stairs, but every time she did, the people would kick her back further back down. Elsa saw the little lamb afraid, abandoned, and rejected, and reached down to the bottom of the stairs to pick her up in her arms. Then she heard the voice of the Lord saying,

"Elsa, the little lamb is Andrea; will you pick her up in your arms and love her? Will you love her for Me?"

My heart was beating fast at the sound of her phone ringing, and at the uncertainty that lingered around me.
"Hello?"
"Elsa, it's me, Andrea. I was wondering . . ."

And before I could say another word, with a tone of excitement in her voice, she said,
"Andrea, where are you? I will pick you up right now! Just tell me where you are! I will come and get you right now!"

Surprised at her excitement and willingness to help me, I gave her my location. She picked me up immediately.

Tia Elsa

Tia Elsa was different from anyone I had ever met. She was happy, and always had a positive outlook to life, no matter the situation or circumstances, which I found strange.

She took pride in decorating her home and keeping it nice and clean, with a warm and cozy feel. Even though I was only fourteen-years-old, I loved the way she took care of her home.

As the weeks rolled by, Elsa and I would watch television, talk, laugh and giggle until the early hours of the morning. I knew staying up late was a sacrifice she made for me, as she had to be up early in the morning with her kids—and for that I loved her even more.

I could be myself with her. She was not critical or judgmental. She did speak her mind, and I liked that, because it showed me she was human just like me, and I could trust her.

While in her company, I found myself often wishing she was my mother, because her conduct toward me said loud and clear that she loved me, just as I was, even in my moments of insanity.

The Bond

I had been off the streets for a few weeks when I was invited to a party by a Canadian girl whom I had previously met in the Spanish church. This is where I met Nero.

We began dating soon after meeting, and around the same time I began feeling sick. Elsa asked me if I could be pregnant.

Sex and how babies were made were topics I had never discussed with anyone before, so I was naive to the fact that I could have gotten pregnant from being sexually intimate.

Days passed, and I continued getting sick. Elsa told my mom, and Mom took me to the doctor for a checkup.

Afterwards, the doctor had Mom and I sit in her office, and her words came as a complete shock:

"You're pregnant!"

In disbelief, I blurted out words that should never be spoken by a teenager:

"But how?"

The doctor gave me a surprised look and said,

"You actually don't know?"

Mom immediately began scolding me in Spanish, telling me how much of a disgrace I was, and how much shame I had brought the family—and now this.

She and the doctor immediately began discussing a schedule for an abortion.

While they spoke, something unexpected happened.

Bond in the Womb

As I was waiting for Mom and the Doctor to choose my fate, I got lost in thought. I looked down at my tummy where I guessed the baby would be, and placed both hands on the area. As I did, I was suddenly in a trance, surrounded with warm feelings of love for the little baby inside of my womb—and with a strong desire to protect it! However, the good feelings were cut short by my mother's harsh words.

"You're having an abortion!"

A wave of sadness came over me as we drove back home. Mom would not allow me to go back to Elsa's and have her find out about my condition and announce it to the church, thus bringing more shame to the family.

When I walked into the house, I felt like a stranger. Everyone was staring at me, not knowing what to say. My younger sister approached me and gave me a hug. But feeling out of place and uncomfortable with everyone's stares, I headed straight to the unfinished basement, where I could be alone with my thoughts and feelings.

I still wonder what I was thinking when I headed to the basement instead of my bedroom upstairs. I guess it felt safer, than being around my family.

I was sitting at the bottom of the stairs looking into the darkness when I was suddenly transported back to a time just over a year earlier when I was still attending the Spanish church.

Flashback . . .
I remember it well. At church, I had joined a two-week prayer chain, devoting one hour every day to praying for the church. I remembered how I had come down to this very basement, faithfully, for two weeks, carrying my clock, to make sure I would finish right on time. Every so many minutes, I would turn to look at the clock and, to my disappointment, notice that only a few minutes had passed. Yes, a part of me was doing it religiously, but also out of love for my church family— and it was love that allowed me to endure each hour every day for those two weeks.

Back to the Present . . .
And as I sat there, at the bottom of the stairs, it hit me: what had I been thinking, volunteering my time to pray for people who had hurt me and turned their backs on me? But just as quickly, I knew the answer in my heart: I did it out of love.

I got up from the stairs and walked over to the very same spot I had prayed on for those two weeks.
I knelt down and the moment my knees hit the ground, it was like a dam opened up inside of me, and I began to cry hard, with years of pain, erupting in three words,
"God HELP ME!"

Suddenly, I was in a vision, with light all around me, and I could hear the voice of God saying,
"Andrea. . . My daughter, you will have a little girl. She will learn from you and you will learn from her. Do not be afraid! Because I am with you, and I, the Lord,

will take care of both of you! Go upstairs and get your bible. I will give you a word to hold onto."

I ran upstairs, excited to find my long-lost bible, believing and expecting that God had a word for me. I picked it up from the night table, blew the dust off, and opened it randomly, allowing my fingers to land wherever God wanted them to.

The Bible opened up to Acts 18:9, 10:
"One night the Lord spoke to Paul in a vision, and said, 'Do not be afraid; keep on speaking, do not be silent. For I am with you, and no one is going to attack and harm you, because I have many people in this city.'"

As I read God's word, I knew God was speaking to me. Strength and courage came upon me to stand up for my baby, my baby girl!

God was promising me that He would protect us. I had nothing and no one to fear; and neither should my family.

I hurried down the stairs with this new courage that had come upon me, and with my bible in my hands, feeling God's tangible presence upon me.

My whole family just happened to be sitting in the living room together, conversing—probably about my present state—and when I appeared they fell silent. I stood in front of them in complete confidence, and my words began to flow.

"I have heard from God in a vision. I am to keep the baby! God says I will have a little girl, and I am not to be afraid, and neither should you, or fear what people will think or say, because God has got a lot of His own people in this city!"

I then read the word God had given me in the Bible.

When I was finished, my family stared back at me, speechless, not able to utter a word, which was yet another miracle in itself.

Nothing else was said.

During my eighth month of pregnancy, I got kicked in the stomach and rolled down the stairs. I landed at the bottom, in pain and unable to breathe. My parents took me to the hospital immediately, warning me not to say a word about what really happened, but to simply say that I fell. Not wanting to bring harm to the family, I did just that. At the hospital, the baby and I were checked thoroughly, and we were both fine.

It was clear that God's hand of protection was upon me during my pregnancy, as God not only protected me from this incident, but from my parents. As they were kind, and attentive to my pregnant condition, making me feel like I mattered. Even when the strange cravings came, if we didn't have it in the house, dad would go and buy it.

The last few months of my pregnancy, my parents became excited about the baby who was about to be born. Mom would buy baby girl's clothes every so often, and every time she came home with the purchases, she would ask me, "Andrea, are you *sure* it's going to be a girl?"

"Yes! God said it's a girl!"

The Promise

I began having labor pains on Friday, January 9. On my way to the hospital, I asked Mom, "Is this how bad the pains will get? Because if it is, I can do this, no problem!"

Mom said, "Just a little bit more."

Within hours, this fifteen-year-old girl was screaming and punching anything and everything in sight, including the nurses. They hated me—and that's probably why when they injected the epidural needle, they missed my spine all together, and therefore the much-needed pain relief never came.

I suffered for two long days. Then finally, on Sunday evening, my baby was born. I gave birth to a baby girl, *just as God had promised*!

Throughout my pregnancy, I had searched out many girl names, but hadn't decided on one. As I held my baby girl in my arms and wondered what her name would be, I was reminded of a *promise* I had once made a friend back home in Santiago.

Flashback

My friend lived across the street from my house with her sister and father. She was eighteen years old, beautiful, and always dressed fashionably. One day, she invited me into her house. I sat politely on the edge of the sofa, in awe of the beauty of her home, from the large French glass doors that welcomed me in to the beautiful, white floral sofa I sat upon to the unique paintings decorating the walls. Dressing the windows were beautiful sheer curtains that danced gracefully at the touch of a summer breeze coming in. A glass vase filled with fresh-cut flowers, probably plucked from their garden, stood on a dark, thick, polished hardwood table. For being given such a privilege, I felt eternally grateful to Daisy, and I said to her,

"When I grow up and get married and have a little girl, I will name her Daisy... just like you. I promise!"

With a kind smile Daisy said, "That's nice."

Back to the Present

Her name would be Daisy Andrea, for indeed she was a beautiful *promise* from Heaven, to me.

Marriage at Sixteen

Nero and I were married. I was only sixteen years old. From the start, our relationship was tumultuous. He held a job only here and there. He began cheating on me, and when caught, he would beg for my forgiveness.

I soon began finding drugs on him and, having no clue of their value or whether he was selling them, I would flush them down the toilet, not wanting them in the house or near my baby. This infuriated him, and he would retaliate violently against me. After the assault, he would disappear for days, weeks, even months.

Andrea Edwards

Depression

Feelings of depression, loneliness, and worthlessness hung over me like a dark cloud, along with suicidal thoughts. But I did my best to cope, as my baby needed me. Nevertheless, there were moments when I felt so much pain, that I would grab a steak knife, and start cutting my arms until blood would spill.

By the time I turned seventeen, I was still looking after my baby girl on my own, in my own apartment, with the help of government assistance for which I was thankful. I got my own bank account, paid my rent (always on time) and went grocery shopping with my daughter by my side.
I thrived in having responsibilities, and met them well. Nevertheless, loneliness and depression hung over me.
Mom and Dad would come over and help me with my baby, and I was grateful for this because I was desperate for help and company. I went out of my way to welcome and attend my parents well, and took joy in preparing meals for us all. But along with the help, their constant hurtful words of judgment and disapproval had returned since having my baby. In Mom's eyes, I couldn't do anything right, and knowing that weighed heavy on my heart.

One night as I sat alone in my living room watching television and weeping, as I usually did after putting my baby to sleep, Nero showed up unannounced, as he always did. He stayed for two or three days, and then left.

Not long afterwards I found out I was pregnant with his baby. I was scared and devastated at the thought of having to care for another baby, alone.

Chapter Seven
Give Your Tears to Jesus

Tia Elsa began attending a new church, Pastor Olea's Spanish church, and she began picking me and Daisy up every Sunday.

Once I got to church, I would take Daisy to the nursery and go to the sanctuary to sit in the last pew, where I wouldn't be noticed. As I knew the unwelcome tears would come, brought on by the constant pain I felt in my heart.

One Sunday right after the service ended, the pastor stepped down from the pulpit and came toward me rather quickly before I had a chance to rush out of the sanctuary as I always did. He knelt down beside me and said, "Andrea, every time I see you sitting back here, you're always crying. Have you ever tried giving your tears to Jesus? Give your tears to Jesus." He said.

I went home not giving much thought to his words. When evening came, I put Daisy to sleep and then went to the living room where I usually sat alone, and cried, as I always did. Then, suddenly, like a warm breeze entering through an open window, the pastor's words came to my mind: "Give your tears to Jesus."

And I understood as clear as day what his words meant: to give Jesus my pain.

Instantly, I got down on my knees, still weeping, and raised my hands to Jesus and began worshiping Him through the pain. I said,

"Jesus, if you do not want Nero in my life; then take him away from my heart, and heal my pain!"

Suddenly, while my tears were still falling and my hands were still lifted up in worship, I saw and felt the Lord's hand reaching down from above, entering into my heart, and taking all the pain away.

The pain was instantly gone! All of it was gone!

Jesus heard my cry, and healed my broken heart, instantly and supernaturally!

While this was happening, the Lord also revealed to me that the baby in my tummy was yet another baby girl.

I was filled with excitement and love for her! I got up from the floor with my hands on my tummy, dancing and rejoicing at the freedom I felt.

I had to share my joy with someone, so I went to see my baby girl, who was sleeping peacefully, looking like the little angel she was. I kissed her rosy cheeks, and whispered in her ear, "Daisy, Jesus just healed my heart! And you're going to have a baby sister!"

I continued dancing, rejoicing around my apartment for a long while after, and eventually I went to sleep, sweetly.

The sadness that had been in me for so many years was gone. However, that night was not over yet. God was about to confirm what He had just done.

Confirmation

I went to sleep, but at about three o'clock in the morning I was awakened by the sound of my apartment buzzer. I got up to answer, knowing full well who it would be: Nero. He was the only one who would appear randomly at such hours. I had not seen him in months, and if it had been any other day, I would have let him in, like I always did. However, my feelings for him had vanished; they were instantly erased that very night. All that lingered in my heart for him was pity for the choices he was making.

"Andrea! Let me in!" he yelled when I answered the intercom.

"No," I answered.

Sounding shocked, he begged me to let him in, but my mind was made up. He was not coming in!

Somehow he got into the building and began knocking on my door—loudly. He demanded that I open the door and threatened to break it down if I didn't. He thought I had a man in the house—and he was right! I *did* have a man in the house, and a powerful man at that! His name was Jesus!

Once again, I firmly told him to leave or I would call the police. He laughed mockingly and said,

"You won't call the police! Just open the door or I'll break it down!"

I called the police and Nero was taken away.

I had a new strength in me, and I liked it.

The Prophecy

I continued attending church with Tia Elsa. She always sat in the front pew, and would always ask me to sit up front with her. I always declined, in part because I believed that the front pews were reserved for the really good people; not for people like me.

However, the Sunday following my supernatural experience with God, I had a newfound confidence and strength within me, so I accepted her offer without any hesitation, never suspecting what was about to take place.

While everyone was worshiping the Lord in song, a lady began prophesying out loud in a strange tongue that I didn't understand. The church became silent and after a few minutes, the pastor announced from the pulpit that the Lord had a message for someone in the church, and encouraged everyone to begin praying. I felt a sense of panic, and whispered to Tia Elsa,

"For some reason I feel like the lady is going to come over to me!"

"Nonsense!" she whispered.

I told Tia Elsa that I was going downstairs because I felt afraid. Elsa quickly grabbed me by the arm and whispered,

"Andrea, don't be silly; you're not going anywhere!"

I turned back to look in the lady's direction, and to my horror, she began walking right out of her pew with her eyes closed, heading toward the front, still speaking in the strange tongue. I thought that God must definitely be guiding her in order for her to walk with her eyes closed.

When she got to the front, she turned in our direction, and I went into panic mode! I sat down and placed my head between my knees, put my hands over my head, and closed my eyes tightly, begging God to keep the lady away from me. But just as I had suspected, the lady came right to me and placed her hands on my head. The pastor encouraged the whole church to continue praying, and he came down from the pulpit, asking his deacon leaders to join him. They all put their hands on my head. I was completely surrounded, and thought that God was about to punish me now, just like my parents had often warned me.

My view of God, though He had shown up supernaturally in my life just days prior, was still highly distorted.

While everyone had their hands on my head, I was shaking in fear, begging God to spare me from whatever punishment He was ready to execute.

Just then, the pastor began translating the lady's strange tongue into what apparently were the words of God.

"Andrea, do not be afraid. God loves you, and He is with you! He has called you and chosen you and will use you mightily to bring many to Himself. His name will be glorified through you!"

More was said, but I don't clearly recall word for word. Nevertheless, I couldn't believe what my ears were hearing. Didn't God know who I was? The rejected girl that no one wanted? Feeling confused, not truly comprehending what had just happened, I was glad and grateful when it was over.

When the service ended, people in the church began gathering around me, congratulating me for the word God had given me. I returned their hugs and handshakes with mixed emotions, feeling highly favored and yet so unworthy.

I continued attending church faithfully every Sunday and began getting involved, helping the older ladies with the kitchen preparations and serving. Some of them would laugh and comment as to why I was in the kitchen helping, when I was only young and should be with the youth instead. Though I was only seventeen, I didn't feel like a youth; I felt like an adult, and when I helped in the kitchen and served the people, I was truly doing it from my heart, out of thankfulness to God for His goodness and mercy over me.

The Pastors

Right after the prophecy, the pastor and his wife began visiting me in my apartment, taking me under their wings as a spiritual mom and dad. At first I felt nervous, as I wasn't used to having kindness extended, and at such length.

I will never forget my first few attempts to cook for them.

I burned the food each time. After a few visits, I bought a pizza, thinking surely I wouldn't burn that. Well, I burned that, too, leaving it in the oven too long. After that, every time they came to visit they would call me the day before, letting me know not to bother cooking, and that they would be bringing supper for all of us to eat. I felt a bit embarrassed, knowing it was because they didn't want to eat my burned food. Nevertheless, I still cooked something, and if I didn't burn it, I would add it to our meal.

My Friend Liz

At church, I became friends with a girl named Liz. As our friendship grew, I thought that Liz was the luckiest girl in the world. Her parents praised her constantly, and boasted of her many school accomplishments and achievements to everyone in church. She was also beautiful and always dressed according to the latest fashion.

I, on the other hand, felt like I had nothing in common with her. I had been kicked out of schools. My parents didn't approve of me in any way. I wore used clothes, and even though I seemed to turn every boy's head my way, my self-esteem was at its lowest. In fact, it was so low that even a glance of myself in a mirror revealed that the pretty little girl I had seen staring back at me from the hotel mirror in Chile six years ago had vanished. All I saw now was the negative *words* I had been labeled with for so many years.

One day, my good friend Carlos, whom I had met in the previous church, was visiting with us, and noticed Liz bossing me around. He said to me,
"Why do you let her treat you like that?"

Liz was bossy, and appeared rude on the surface, but down deep she had a good heart. Nevertheless, Carlos' words surfaced hidden feelings within me. I was jealous and envious of her, and so had accepted what I thought was her rightful mistreatment of me.
Nevertheless, our teen friendship continued, and Liz became eagerly excited with me about my baby girl coming soon. She visited me at home often, and we

searched together for baby girl names. We found the name Cristal, and I liked it. It spoke of transparency, purity, and heavenly beauty.

The name Sara was one of my favorites, because I had heard a sermon from the pastor about Abraham and Sara. The pastor had told us of their love and respect for one another, and it was something I deeply admired and desired.

Kicked Out

Fully pregnant and only weeks before giving birth, Liz and I got into a heated argument, and we both ended up in the pastor's office, with the pastor and his wife present.

I was interrogated, made to feel as if I was the guilty one, and probably was, as I still harbored the same feelings toward Liz. My pride got in the way when they zeroed in on me.

Feeling hurt and angry, I began swearing at Liz right in front of the pastors, not caring who heard me.

In retaliation, Liz began yelling and swearing back at me. Then all of a sudden in the midst of our yelling match, the pastor's wife jumped out of her chair and turned toward me, fuming, and ordered me to shut up. What came next I could have never imagined. Pointing with her hand toward the door in a loud and angry tone, she said,

"Andrea! I want you to leave the church now! Leave now, and don't come back!"

I stared at her in shock. I couldn't believe what I was hearing. She repeated herself.

"Leave the church now, and don't come back!"

Just then, Elsa, who had been standing outside the office door listening along with other ladies from the church, burst into the office in my defense. But I was already on my way out, feeling the horrible pains of rejection in my heart that had come back with a vengeance. I went to pick Daisy up from the nursery and left the church.

Elsa eventually came out of the church, fuming and ranting about my mistreatment.

As we drove home, I held my baby close to me and wept so hard, unable to control the flood of tears coming from the pit of my stomach.

I had come to love, respect, and even trust the pastors, and never imagined that they would break my heart so deeply.

Through the pain, I spoke in anger, and vowed never to trust anyone, or set foot in a church again, as long as I lived.

"Andrea," said Tia Elsa, sounding alarmed. "Please don't say that!"

But the pain within me was speaking.

Stronghold of Fear

When my younger sister heard what had happened, she came over to keep me company in my apartment. That same Sunday, we went downtown, while Mom took care of Daisy. As we were window shopping, we randomly decided to go see a movie. All the movies had already begun playing, and given their options, I felt strongly that we weren't supposed to watch any of them. But I was driven by my flesh and was ignoring the voice within me, which was the voice of the Holy Spirit helping me.

I picked the movie that had been playing for the shortest time—not a good choice. The movie turned out to be about a woman who was being tormented by an evil spirit. Through the whole movie, I felt uneasy because I knew this stuff was real to some degree. I tried to convince myself that it was just a movie, but I was sure glad when it was over.

I awoke that night to the sound of my closet door sliding open. I turned on the light to see what the noise was about, and everything looked to be intact, other than the closet door being partly opened. I tried to ignore the feeling of fear I felt, and went back to bed. Just when I was dozing off, the sound of loud noises startled me awake again.

My heart started pounding fast and I became paralyzed with fear. I tried calling out to my sister, who was sleeping in the other room, but my voice wouldn't come out. Finally, after a few tries, I let out a yell calling her name, and she rushed into my room wondering what was happening.

When the lights came on, I looked in the closet and realized that some of the things from the top shelf had fallen down. *But how?* I wondered. My closet was a bit messy, piled up with stuff that could easily have tumbled down any other day, but it didn't. *Why tonight?*

I knew it didn't happen by chance.

And it wasn't until years later, that I came to understand that the devil was able to execute one of his plan's in my life that night, because I had given him territory in my heart.

I had been the one to open the door and give grounds to the enemy when I had spoken in anger to never set foot in a church again, and when I disobeyed God's leading to not go see that movie.

I am not justifying the pastors wrongdoing, I'm just being accountable for my actions, and taking ownership of my mistakes.

God knew the devil's plans for me that night, and He tried to protect me. But I disobeyed His leading.

So the enemy's plans against me succeeded, and a stronghold of *fear* was placed in my life that night, that would torment me for years to come every time I would try to pray or read my bible. So I did less of both.

My Baby Girl!

Spring arrived, and only weeks before my eighteenth birthday, I gave birth to a beautiful baby girl just as the Lord had said. I named her Cristal Sara.

The pastors came to pay me a brief visit at the hospital. They brought me a card and admired my new baby girl.

I welcomed them, but the air between us was thick. Nevertheless, I would never forget their kindness to me, short-lived as it had been.

But one day the seeds of love God had planted in my heart would grow.

While I slept in the hospital that night, I had an unknown visitor leave an unsigned card on my night table.

It quoted Proverbs 17:17:

"A friend loves at all times."

I read the card over and over again, feeling in my heart that it had to have been from Liz. The gesture meant a lot to me, as I'd grieved the loss of our friendship.

When I got home, I framed the card, and I keep it nearby to this day as a reminder of a lesson painfully Learned.

Chapter Eight
Violent Pursuit

Nero was now fully involved in a life of crime, and even with a restraining order in place, he began a violent pursuit to kill me if I didn't take him back.

The police in the Londonderry area knew who he was because he was also suspected of being involved in a few bank robberies and other crimes. So when they received a call from me, they'd show up within minutes and surround the building.

One night while I slept, Nero broke into my second-floor apartment through a sliding window in my living room. To my horror, I awoke with him on top of me, choking me. My body was pinned under him, and I couldn't move.

I struggled to get away, while he threatened to kill me and accused me of having another man in my life. He thought that was why I wasn't taking him back. He'd threatened to kill me for a while, but I had never taken his threats seriously. However, Nero wasn't thinking straight; he was clearly under the influence of drugs and alcohol. With his weight on top of me and his hands tightening around my neck, I struggled to breathe and began to panic, thinking that he was going to kill me, after all.

I cried out to Jesus for help and, instantly, my one-hundred-pound frame became empowered with supernatural strength, and I was able to throw Nero off me. He went hurtling off the bed, against the wall, and landed on the ground. I jumped up and ran to a neighbor's apartment where I was able to call the police.

While I waited for the police to arrive, I was worried for my girls. Nero had never done anything to hurt them before. The times he had spent with the girls, he was loving and attentive to them; however, he was under some dark narcotic influence.

I had to go back, even though I was advised not to by the police. I had to go back for my girls' sake.

Knowing in the back of my mind that the police were right behind me on their way to save us, I opened the door to my apartment. It was dark and dreadfully quiet; only the sound of my heartbeat pounding a mile a minute could be heard.

As I slowly crept in through the door, in the distant shadows of the hallway, I could see Daisy sitting quietly, rubbing her eyes, looking sleepy and unharmed. I picked her up, settled her on my hip, and went to get Cristal.

I picked Cristal up from her crib and began walking down the dark hallway with both my girls balancing on my hips, trembling in fear that at any moment Nero would appear from the darkness and attack me.

Just when I was ready to reach the front door and walk out, it slammed shut in my face, and Nero emerged from behind it! Terrified, I tried behaving as calmly and submissively as possible, knowing that the police would be arriving at any moment.

Nero, with the obvious appearance of someone using drugs and losing his mind, began hitting my face, not caring that I had the girls in my arms. Just then, a team of police officers burst in through the doors at full force, grabbed Nero from behind, and pulled him out of the apartment into the hallway.

Nero was highly trained in martial arts. Weighing a-hundred-and-eighty-five pounds of muscle, he was not going down without a fight, and the police—having dealt with him in the past—knew they had a challenge on their hands. Finally, after a long struggle out in the hallway, the police were able to restrain him, handcuff him, and take him away.

Nero went to jail, but his stay was short, and his threats continued.

I lived in constant fear that he would reappear and hurt me.

Then one day, I was coming into my apartment building with my girls and a three-year-old boy whom I babysat, when I suddenly heard a strange noise coming from down the hallway. I was holding Cristal in my left arm, and Daisy and the little boy were holding hands next to me while

I nervously tried to find the key to open my apartment door. Then I heard the noise again. I turned to look down the hallway, and saw someone's head peeking out of the laundry room. It was Nero! My hands began shaking as I desperately tried to identify the correct key, buried among my many key charms, to open the apartment door. Suddenly, to my horror, Nero came out of the laundry room and charged toward us like an angry bull in a stampede, yelling,

"I am going to kill you!"

Next thing I knew, he punched me in the face, and I collapsed to the ground with the taste of blood in my mouth and the sound of the children crying.

Then Nero suddenly stared at me, with a look of shock mixed with fear, while I lay on the ground, perhaps reacting to the sight of blood on my face. In a state of confusion and even remorse for what he'd done, he took off running out of the building.

I rushed into my apartment and called the police.

Eventually, Nero was arrested and spent some time in jail again. While he was incarcerated, I moved to where I wouldn't be found. It took a while to be able to live without the fear of him reappearing out of nowhere, but that was to be the last incident.

A decade or so later Nero and I reconnected; he gave his heart to Jesus, and got his life straighten out, and we both forgave all. Until this day, we remain friends.

That's what the Lord can do.

As my life settled from all the chaos, I applied to become a Canadian citizen. I studied and answered all the questions correctly. The judge was proud of me, and warmly said,

"You should be very proud of yourself young lady; you have answered all the questions correctly, and now you are a Canadian citizen!"

Then he proceeded to say,

"Did you know that most Canadians don't even know half of the answers to the questions you were asked today?"

I was very surprised at his statement, and at the same time, I felt a sense of accomplishment.

My Friend

Around the same time, I met a man named Eugene who worked for the railroad. We began visiting in the evenings.

Our visits were short and always took place in the kitchen. Friendship and company was all I wanted.

During our visits, I found myself often speaking about Jesus, even surprising myself. Eugene accepted Jesus into his heart, and began reading his bible every day.

Around the same time, Mom and Dad decided that they were moving to Ontario, and Mom said they were taking Daisy with them.

The separation was painful for the three of us. We shed many tears. Our hearts were deeply wounded.

A year later, I moved to Ontario with Cristal and Eugene, and reunited with Daisy. When we saw each other, the three of us ran, and held each other tight, and cried.

Before the move to Ontario, I filed for divorce. I was nervous through the process, believing something would go wrong and prevent it from happening. I also feared that I was breaking a serious commandment in God's eyes. Nevertheless, everything went smoothly, and after all the legal procedures were properly executed, the divorce was finalized. I was no longer married.

The Visitation

We found a home in Oshawa, Ontario. On Waverly street to be exact. One Sunday afternoon in October of 1987, while my girls, my younger sister, and Eugene sat at the kitchen table, I began singing a worship song I remembered in Spanish.

"Te Exaltaré, Mi Dios Mi Rey." ("I will exalt you, My Lord, My King.")

As I continued singing, God's presence came over me so strongly that tears of joy began streaming down my face.

I felt as if there was a river flowing through me, cleansing me from heavy burdens within. I encouraged my sister and Eugene to join me in worshiping God, and as they did, the tangible presence of God filled the room.

I went to sleep that night never imagining what was about to take place.

The Angel of the Lord

Monday morning, I awoke to someone calling my name softly.

"Andrea."

I turned my face and looked toward my left and saw that the clock read 6:00. Then I heard my name again:

"Andrea"

I turned around to face the ceiling, and there, to my amazement, was an angel!

He was huge, taking over the hall ceiling and wall. His face was soft. His eyes were radiant, like light. He had long, flowing hair the color of light. He wore a long, white, flowing gown, with a thick golden belt around his waist.

He also had what appeared to look like wings, and light shone brightly around him and through him.

For the third time, he spoke my name. He said,

"Andrea, raise the girls in the ways of the Lord, for they have been chosen by God to do His will. Don't worry about Eugene, for God will take care of him. God is with you, and He will lead you and guide you in the way you should go."

When the angel finished speaking, he vanished from the room.

I got up from the bed immediately, and ran downstairs in excitement to where my younger sister was sleeping on the sofa. She was already semi-awake, so I began sharing the angel's visitation. My sister's exact words were:

"You know, I believe you, because it's as if I could feel and almost see the angel's presence."

Testament Book Shop

That very same day, I went searching for a Christian bookstore, desiring to follow the Lord's leading. Amazingly, I found one right around the corner from where I lived: Testament Book Shop. I bought all kinds of Christian children's music and storybooks there, and we began listening to the songs and learning them by heart.

I also began reading the storybooks to the girls every day, ending each night holding hands in prayer.

The fear that had once lingered every time I tried to pray was gone.

The months passed, and our Christian story bookshelf grew rapidly. The reading, praying, and singing to the Lord continued for many more years to come.

I didn't see the big picture then, but God's Word was being instilled in all of us, planting seeds in the garden of our hearts that one day would sprout to maturity.

One of the messages from the angel was not to worry about Eugene. I didn't understand then, but in a year, I would.

In the meantime, God was simply being Himself, acting upon His nature—being a Father to the fatherless.

Psalms 68:5 "Father of the fatherless and protector . . ."

Healing

The following year, in the summer of 1988, I was working at a construction site dry-walling when suddenly I began having back pain. At first, I ignored the pain, imagining that I must have pulled a muscle with all the heavy lifting my five-foot-four, hundred-pound frame was doing. But the pain got worse as the hours passed, and I ended up in the emergency room at the nearest hospital.

The emergency waiting room was packed, and the pain became increasingly worse while I waited, to the extent that I was bent over in a fetal position, crying loudly, probably frightening and upsetting everyone.

Finally, I was called in and put through some tests. When the tests came back, the doctor said I had kidney stones and he wasn't sure if they were able to pass on their own, because they were so large. Surgery would probably be needed.

I lay in agony on the hospital bed, and the bible stories I'd been reading to my girls began to play in my mind, particularly, "The Miracles of Jesus."
Jesus healed all those who asked Him and believed Him to do it. All of them were healed! So surely He could heal me.

I lifted my hands and began worshiping God through the pain, asking Him to heal me; expecting Him to do it.

The minutes passed, and I continued worshiping through the pain, and suddenly, it happened!

My arms were lifted high in worship when, all of a sudden, God's presence came upon me in the form of warmth that entered through my hands and moved through my arms into my body. The warmth continued moving through me, into my legs and out through my feet, removing all the pain with it. The pain was gone! Completely gone! I was healed!

I lay there, overwhelmed and amazed at God's supernatural healing touch!

Just then, a nurse entered the room, holding something in her hands. I asked her what it was, and she said, "Morphine, for the pain."

I had no knowledge of what morphine was, and as she explained, I exclaimed in excitement,

"I don't need that anymore! You see, I was asking Jesus to heal me, and He did! Jesus healed me! I have no more pain! It's all gone!"

She paused for a few seconds, looking confused at my words, and then said,

"I have doctor's orders to give this to you."

Not desiring to cause trouble, I let her give me the medication, but as soon as she was gone, I got out of the bed and began walking down the hallway.

I saw the doctor who had been treating me, and began telling him about the miracle I had just received.

He stared back at me speechless and with a look of confusion. It was obvious he didn't understand what I was talking about, either.

He looked toward the nurse who was in charge of me, and asked if she had given me the medication. She said, yes.

So the doctor immediately attributed my story to the painkillers having numbed the pain, and said,

"Young lady, if you leave now, you will be back in two hours, screaming in pain, because you have large kidney stones that will have to be surgically removed!"

Confident within me that Jesus had healed me, I said,

"No, doctor. I will not be back, because you see, Jesus really did heal me!"

I left the hospital and went straight to my parents' house to share what had happened. Dad listened attentively while sitting on the sofa rubbing his beard. Mom listened nervously while she washed the dishes. She doubted my story and told me to go back to the hospital.

When I finished sharing, Dad got up from the sofa and said, "Well, if God healed you, then God healed you! We will not worry or talk about it any longer!"

I was surprised and encouraged by Dad's faith.

I never went back to the hospital.

The following year, Eugene's dad passed away and his mom fell ill so he moved back to Alberta.

It was then that I understood the angel's words concerning Eugene.

God was going to take care of us.

Nevertheless, the move was sudden and very painful for the three of us. He had become my best friend and a father to the girls—and suddenly it was all over. He packed up and left for good.

I also understood that he needed to go for the simple reason that we were not married, but were pretending to live as husband and wife without the sexual intimacy.

He needed a wife, not just a best friend to live with.

The girls and I missed him terribly and cried every day for months.

Without his contribution, we could no longer afford the house we lived in, so we moved into a basement apartment. At the same time, we were hit with yet another heartbreaker: we had to get rid of our dog because our new landlords didn't want any pets.

The months slowly rolled by, and I was barely surviving emotionally. Feelings of unworthiness and loneliness plagued me, and I knew I wasn't the only one hurting—my girls were, too, and I didn't know how to help them.

Out of obedience to God, I kept reading our bible storybook every night and praying a repetitive prayer with my girls. It was the same one I prayed alone when I went to sleep every night, perceiving it as an urgent prayer:

"Dear Jesus, forgive me for my sins, cover the girls and me with Your precious blood, and fill us with Your love and wisdom. In Jesus's name, amen!"

I knew Mom attended a Spanish church every Sunday, so with that in mind, I began taking the girls to her place most weekends, knowing she would take them to church. Still, it was a battle every time I dropped them off because my girls didn't want to stay with Mom.

Mom wouldn't help the situation, as she would begin yelling at me in front of the girls, saying that I was a horrible mother and that I didn't love my daughters or I wouldn't be leaving them behind. My girls cried even louder as they heard the hurtful words, and our separation for the weekend was a stressful one.

Chapter Nine
Death to Life

On the weekends, I began hanging out with a friend at a sports lounge. I played pool, as I had done during my street days, and as I got better, I joined a league and played tournaments with some of the best in town. I also sang karaoke and entered into some local competitions just to pass the time, even winning once in a while.

However, winning always came with a superficial happiness that faded within seconds. The prize was usually a trophy or a stuffed animal that I would shamefully hide when I got home, as they weren't symbols of positive achievement in my life, but only reminders of the pain and emptiness in my heart I was trying to fill.

At the end of 1989, I re-connected with Roger Edwards, whom I had met back in 1987.

We began dating, seeing each other mostly on the weekends. On weeknights after my girls were in bed, Roger and I would spend hours on the phone talking or simply listening to each other breathe. Somehow, knowing that we were near each other was a comfort to both of us. We dreamt of becoming a family, spending our lives together in love, and raising the girls together. But at the same time, my heart ached with sadness because I believed a lie that had been repeated to me by my parents, that I could never be married again because I had once been married and divorced. This was apparently God's law, and could not be broken.

Nevertheless, I continued dating Roger secretly, until one day I heard the words my heart longed to hear:

"Andrea, I love you." Then I heard them again, and knew he meant them from the bottom of his heart.

"I love you, Andrea, and I want to spend the rest of my life with you!"

They were words that should have brought me joy, but instead they frightened me, and I realized at that moment that I had to back away. If I kept seeing him, it would only make things worse for both of us, and I had to stop tormenting my heart—and his—with dreams that could never be.

I distanced myself from Roger, and as I did, I sank deeper into a pit of depression that was about to cost me my life.

It was 1994, and for the past four years I had fallen far from grace, choosing one wrong choice after another. Depression and hopelessness were my constant companions. I began visiting the self-help section in the book stores, buying books about the New Age movement and astrology. I read and studied them and began putting their teachings into practice, but they weren't helping. I called the psychic lines, hoping they would give me direction for my life, but it was all a waste of time and money, and only plunged me deeper into a dark life of despair.

Our financial situation was poorly. We barely got by.

My job allowed me a budget of fifty dollars for groceries and needs for the week, after rent and bills were paid.

Mom and Dad began bringing me groceries every so often, which was helpful, and I was thankful. However, along with their help came their hurtful judgment and condemnation, reminding me of what a useless mother and human being I was in this world. Their words cut deep, and sent me even deeper into darkness.

My brother, knowing our financial struggles, took on the responsibility for the girls' back to school and winter needs for years. He even bought them Wonderland passes for the summer holidays, which they used often.

Over the previous years, my girls and I had visited a church in the area a few times. The nights following our visits, Satan came back with his fear tactics, threatening me not to go back to church and to stop praying altogether or else he would continue to torment me with fear as he had in Edmonton.

I kept away from church, and at the same time deception began playing in my mind, entertaining thoughts of why I even bothered with God when He had rules that I couldn't abide by, rules that were keeping me from happiness, I thought. All I wanted was a family. A husband who would love me and who would love my girls as his own. But apparently, because I had been married when I was sixteen and was now a divorcee, I could never be married again.

As far as I was concerned, God's laws were cruel!

But I was so wrong. I didn't realize the enemy had taken residency in my mind, making God look like my enemy.

Desperate for Happiness

I sat inside a restaurant lounge with a friend, feeling like I had reached a fork in the road and I had to make a decision, on which way to go, quickly.

I looked around, and saw the same people I saw every weekend, and began thinking at how miserable most of them were, if not all, me included. We were all on the same journey, on board in the ship of despair, desperately looking for love.

Thoughts of deception played in my mind. There had to be a better way than God's way, I thought.

I was being deceived by the devil into thinking that God was keeping me from happiness, when in truth He was the very source of happiness and everything good.

"Are you happy with your life?" I asked a friend while we sat observing the crowds around us.

Laughing sarcastically, she answered,
"No, but who cares!?"

I was determined to find a way to be happy , as I was dying inside!

Deceived

When I got home that night, thoughts of deception continued playing in my mind. I didn't want any more rules to restrict me, telling me how to live life. I had always been somewhat of a good girl, never crossing the line of sin too far. Perhaps not putting my values aside had been the problem all along. I didn't want to care anymore. I was broken, depressed, barely surviving emotionally, and desperately wanted a way out!

I stood in the middle of my living room feeling God's strong conviction as I was about to commit sexual sin, when a spirit of rebellion came upon me, and I looked toward heaven and said,

"God, turn your face from me! I want to live life my own way!" And I meant it!

Instantly, I had a vision and saw the image of God's face turning from me—and in such pain—at my request.

I was now officially on my own, or so I thought. Unknowingly, I had just flung the doors of my soul wide open to Satan. His plans were to kill me, immediately!

The Warlock

About the same time, I met an older man close to my father's age who happened to be from Central America. He was friends with a deejay who liked me and had asked me out a couple of times. I refused his requests each time. The deejay introduced me to the older man, who spoke Spanish. The old man was really unattractive.

Upon talking to him, I found out that he was a practicing warlock who had recently arrived in Canada. I didn't know what a warlock was, but I was soon to find out he was the real thing. The deejay's intentions for introducing me to him were self-serving. He was hoping that his friend the warlock would use his powers and make the deejay and me a couple.

The warlock began to tell me that he had powers to make things happen. I was curious to learn more, so I asked him what kind of powers he had. He said, "Powers to change people's lives."

"Where do your powers come from?" I asked.

He laughed arrogantly and said, "From me, of course!"

Even though I had kicked God out of my life, I still believed in Him, and so I said,

"I only know of two powers: God's power and the devil's power. Where do your powers come from?"

Somewhat taken back by my statement and question, he answered nervously,

"Well, some of the powers come from God, of course; and some from me."

Then immediately swerving away from the question, he said,

"Let me come over to your house and I will show you what I can do. I will even show you how to use these powers."

Feeling curious and desperately seeking a way out of my misery, I accepted the warlock's challenge.

The following week, I took an afternoon off work to visit with Mr. Warlock while my girls were in school, not wanting them near him.

He arrived right on time, carrying a small black suitcase. In it were small bottles filled with liquids of some sort. He called them his "work potions."

As we sat at the table, he pulled out an envelope and began showing me pictures of people that he had helped in some way or another.

A young woman's picture got my attention because she was apparently very sick, and couldn't walk. He stated that he was presently working on her. Feeling compassion for the young women in the picture, I began sharing how I had experienced healing—not from man, but from God, and when He'd healed me, He'd healed me right away.

As I was sharing my story, I could see that it was making him uncomfortable. He said,

"I see your belief in God is strong?"

I answered with a confident, yes, but at the same time felt a sadness and shame come over me for having kicked God out of my life. Not wanting to hear more about God, he said, "Let's get started right away."

He began putting his potions on my feet and hands. I watched him in doubt, believing nothing would happen. Then he began chanting something I couldn't make out.

He looked at me and said,

"There is something wrong with you, very wrong, somewhere in this area," pointing toward my body.

Feeling somewhat alarmed, I asked him what it was.

He said, "It's not really clear. It would help if you removed your clothes and I will be able to tell you what it is."

At this point, I realized the guy was nothing more than an old pervert, and as phony as a three-dollar bill.

He tried to convince me that his request was legitimate and simply part of his job. I didn't believe him. I firmly asked him to leave my home right away and stood by the front door, holding it open. He gathered his things and left.

Nevertheless, a heavy evil presence that hadn't been there before lingered behind in the house. I went to wash my hands and feet from the potions, thinking that perhaps there was a connection, but no change came. The evil presence was now upon me.

As the days passed, I became physically ill. I felt fatigued and suffered flu-like symptoms. By the end of the week, the sick feelings had intensified greatly and I felt like my physical strength was being drained out of me.

I got off work early, picked up the girls from school, and went home.

I quickly began preparing dinner for the girls, so I could go and lie down. While cooking, my body was struck with pain. My legs gave way under me, and I dropped to the floor.

Frightened, I dragged myself to my room, which happened to be right beside the kitchen. I crawled into bed, giving my oldest daughter instructions to take care of the food on the stove.

The minutes passed, and the pain and weakness in my body intensified. I wondered if it was due to kidney stones, as I'd just had an episode in March, but the pain felt different. Whatever it was, evil was definitely attached to it.

Feeling concerned, my twelve-year-old daughter decided to call the house doctor, whose number we had posted on the refrigerator in case of an emergency. The doctor came and checked me, but he didn't have any answers. He suggested I be seen at the hospital immediately because my blood pressure was very low, and he left.

The pains in my body became increasingly worse, and I felt a rush of urgency to get to the hospital immediately. But when I tried to stand, my body hit the floor like dead. In desperation and with all the strength I could muster, I crawled to the washroom. When I reached it, all of a sudden, my life was suddenly being sucked right out of me by a dark evil force, and I lost consciousness.

As I lay on the floor unconscious in the physical realm, I was instantly awake and conscious in a realm of total darkness. The presence of evil was all around me. Suddenly, monstrous hands—black, long, and claw-like—appeared out of the darkness and began to pierce through me, digging, pulling, and gouging at my heart.

I immediately realized that the hands were actually pulling at the very person inside of me; they were pulling at my soul. With this cognizance, I understood that I had been the one to give Satan rights to my soul the night I had rejected God by asking Him to turn his face from me, desiring to live life without him.
I also understood I had opened the door to Satan by allowing his servant, the warlock, to put a curse on me.
With this horrible realization, I looked beyond the monstrous hands and saw a black, monstrous-looking creature with a black hood. It was Satan! To my horror and before my very eyes, Satan began violently pulling and claiming what was his—my soul, to take it to HELL!

In utter terror, and in sheer desperation. I cried out in a loud voice, calling on the Name above all names: "JESUSSS!!!!!!!"
Immediately, Jesus came to my rescue! My hands went up in the air, and, with authority, I spoke. I said,
"SATAN, GET YOUR HANDS OFF MY SOUL IN THE NAME OF JESUS!"
Immediately and instantaneously, Satan took his hands off my soul and vanished from my presence!
I was in complete awe at the supernatural power in the name of Jesus!

I ended up regaining consciousness in the emergency hospital gurney. My whole body was shaking uncontrollably, and though I was afraid of what I was experiencing physically, I couldn't stop thinking about what I had just experienced in the supernatural realm and what Jesus had just done for me.

He had saved me from Satan himself!

I realized for the first time in my life that I didn't really know *who* Jesus was, and I desperately wanted to get to know Him. I wanted to know this amazing Jesus who had just saved me from a possible eternity in hell!

After Jesus's manifestation of power, authority, and *love* for me, He had, as you can imagine, my undivided devoted attention.

Chapter Ten
Revelations

I was admitted to hospital and my stay—between that one and another hospital—would last almost two months. I went through all kinds of medical tests. My body ached in pain, and I could barely walk. It seemed that death was after me, and the fear of dying was overwhelming at times. However, one thing I was sure of now: Jesus had saved me. He had rescued me when I called His name, so if I did happen to die at this point, I knew heaven, not hell, would be my destination.

When Roger learned that I was in the hospital, he began visiting me faithfully, bringing me flowers and gifts each time. But my life had completely changed in an instant, and knowing I was risking our friendship, I told him that I was no longer going to be a part of the worldly lifestyle I had been living. I had given my heart to Jesus, and I was going to serve Him with my life.

His response surprised me.

"I don't want the kind of life I am living either," he said. "Andrea, I want you!"

I was saddened by his answer, for I still believed that, because I had once been married, I could never marry again. I told him that I was going to find a church and begin attending it faithfully with my girls, hoping that he would just pull back and move forward with his life.

His answer surprised me once again, and saddened me even more.

"I respect that. And when you do find a church, wait for me. I will go with you."

Roger continued visiting me, and I continued to speak to him about Jesus. He listened attentively, but I thought it was only because of his love for me. I was partly right—but God had a plan for Roger, too.

I had other friends who came to visit me and I will be forever grateful to them because they took the time. But because of what I had experienced, all I wanted to talk about was my Jesus, and this resulted in the loss of a few visits. Nevertheless, to those visitors who read this now, I would like to say that I am forever grateful for you and your efforts to visit me, and I know without any doubt that God planted His seeds of love in you. One day, if they haven't already, those seeds will grow to maturity in your heart, and give you a new and wonderful life!

God's seeds are His Word. His Word never returns void!

"As the rain and the snow come down from heaven, and do not return to it without watering the earth and making it bud and flourish, so that it yields seed for the sower and bread for the eater, so is my word that goes out from my mouth: It will not return to me empty, but will accomplish what I desire and achieve the purpose for which I sent it." —Isaiah 55:10-11

The weeks passed, and I was still very much in pain. I had different kinds of medical specialists treating me, and was still going through all sorts of tests, from early mornings to late afternoons. Doctors assured me that they were working hard at finding the root of my illness. I even saw a psychiatrist who, at the end of our meeting, said,

"It's been a pleasure and a delight speaking with you, and I must say, there is nothing mentally wrong with you. In fact, you're much saner and balanced than most of the people I know!"

I hadn't shared my near-death experience with him—or with anyone, for that matter—as I was still processing what had happened to me myself.

The Promises of God

My older sister surprised me with a visit one day.

I hadn't spoken to or seen her in years. She came into my room holding a book titled, *The Promises of God*. Her visit was short, as she stated that she had only dropped by to give me the book. Still, I was encouraged in my heart that God would one day heal and restore our relationship as sisters.

I held the book in my hands, captured by its title. *The Promises of God*. I began reading it, and discovered that the promises from God were taken from the scriptures in the bible. They were put together in this small book, separated according to their topics and meanings to make it easy to find scripture verses. I thought that whoever had come up with this idea for a book was a genius. It was perfect for a beginner like me! It was just what I needed.

I was surprised at how many promises there were in the bible, and that they were fitting for every situation that anyone in the world could possibly find themselves in. I couldn't put the book down, and began spiritually devouring every promise.

Some of the medical tests came back normal, but my blood pressure was extremely low. This posed a concern for the doctors and was the main reason for my hospitalization.

We Are Spiritual Beings

While I lay in bed one night, two nurses came in to check on me. One of them seemed to be having trouble reading my blood pressure, so she asked the other nurse to come and check the reading. After trying a few times, they both came up with the same reading. Thinking I was asleep, one whispered to the other, "With blood pressure as low as this, you'd think this girl was dead!"

Eventually, they left the room, and I was left alone with my thoughts. If they only knew how true their words had been, for only weeks before, death had come for me. But if I had told anyone this truth, they would surely have thought of me as crazy. Indeed, if I hadn't experienced it myself, I, too, would have had difficulty believing such an incredible, supernatural story.

All of this got me thinking, as I lay there in the darkness of my room, about how many people have indeed been labeled crazy, and even locked up in mental institutions for having had similar experiences. And—even worse—how many are in hell because they didn't call on the name of Jesus.

We are spiritual beings, on an earthly journey. God created us in His image; He is a spirit, and so are we. Real life takes place in the spiritual realm, not in the natural realm.

God was opening my eyes to the spiritual realm, where real life was taking place and where real battles between good and evil were being fought. Most people live their lives completely unaware of such an urgent truth that determines where they will spend eternity, heaven or hell!

The Lord revealed to me that "hell" is the complete absence of God; therefore, it is the very real and tangible presence of absolute and sheer EVIL.

The Enemy Strikes

I felt there was something wrong with the IV on my hand, so I mentioned it to a nurse. She had a quick look and found nothing amiss. But later that night, I awoke to a puddle of blood and two nurses on each side of me changing the IV, my clothes, and my bedding.

It turned out that the IV had been put in incorrectly after all, and the loss of blood had lowered my blood pressure dangerously. Feeling the physical effects of this blood loss in my body, I pulled the sheets over me and trembled, both physically and in fear, as I was aware that the enemy had attempted to strike again. Nevertheless, he had failed, because Jesus was with me, protecting me, just like one of His promises that I was memorizing said in

Hebrews 13:5, 6: *"Never will I leave you; never will I forsake you. So we say with confidence, the Lord is my helper; I will not be afraid. What can man do to me?"*

As I lay in the hospital bed with the sheets over my head, I began calling on Jesus's name, whispering it over and over again, and His tangible presence came and calmed the storm within me, filling me with peace.

I began to understand that God wasn't distant from me. He wasn't far away like I had come to imagine Him to be, sitting somewhere up high with an iron rod, ready to hit me every time I messed up.

No, His arms were always extended to me in love. He was as close as the whisper of His name, Jesus.

Do you find yourself overwhelmed by troubles and pains, and can't see a way out? Say His name: Jesus!!!

He is as close as the whisper of His name, Jesus!

With my sights set on God, I found yet another promise in His scriptures that altogether revolutionized my life:

Mark 11:24. *"Jesus said . . . Therefore I tell you, whatever you ask for in prayer, believe that you have received it, and it will be yours."*

What a promise! What a simple and to-the-point promise, I thought! Jesus was telling me to *ask*, *believe*, and *expect* Him to come through.

I knew God had the power to do supernatural miracles because He had done them in my life before. But, in contradiction, I also falsely believed that He had done enough for me by saving me from Satan's hands, and that I wasn't worthy of any more miracles. God had done His part.

God opened my spiritual eyes and revealed to my heart that the *gift* of salvation included *healing*, and that it was received by faith in Jesus Christ!

It's easy for the believer to believe by *faith* that when we die we will go to heaven. We don't quarrel or worry about that. But when it comes to healing, we doubt His word. Why? I realized that the choice to receive His gift of healing was left up to me.

Do I receive His gift of healing by faith? Or do I reject his gift, as I had rejected Him only weeks before?

How could I deny Jesus again after all He had done for me? I wanted all of Jesus! I asked Jesus to heal me at that moment, believing and expecting Him to come through.

Still in doubt about our heavenly Father desiring to heal us? Think of this: What *good* father in his right mind wouldn't want his child healed if he was sick and suffering?

The word of God says,

"If you then, being evil, know how to give good gifts to your children, how much more will your Father who is in heaven give good things to those who ask Him!"

Matthew 7:11;

Ask, believe, and expect Him to heal you, because healing is indeed God's gift to all who simply believe.

Andrea Edwards

Hospital Conversions

The more the Lord revealed Himself to me, the more I wanted to share Him with everyone.

In the hospital, I met a man in his early thirties who worked for a well-known Toronto newspaper as a comic-strip artist. At first, I wondered if he was a visitor, because he wore his normal day-to-day clothes and didn't appear sick. However, as we became friends, I learned that he had been diagnosed with MS. I felt compassion for him, and shared how Jesus had saved me from death itself. I encouraged him that no matter what diagnosis he was given, Jesus was much bigger than any illness, and even death.

I loaned him the book *Promises of God*, and assured him that all the verses found in that little book were actual promises from God Himself, taken from the bible.

Three days passed before I saw him again. He walked toward me, holding the book in his hand. I could see something different in his eyes that I hadn't before: hope. As he handed me the book, I asked him what he thought about it. His exact words were, "I read it from cover to cover, and it's almost too good to be true."

I could see that God had revealed Himself to him, but I could also see a battle of fear raging within him. Satan was holding him back, preventing him from taking a step toward Jesus. I grabbed hold of his hands, encouraging him to ask Jesus into his heart. He did, as I led him in a prayer of salvation. I know I will see this man again, if not down here on earth, then in heaven one day!

Chapter Eleven
Healing

Days before Christmas, I was let out of the hospital as an outpatient. I still suffered from strange pains and weakness in my body. My legs and feet were constantly breaking out in terrible cold sweats, feeling as though they were being dipped in buckets of ice water. Not knowing what caused it frightened me.

On Christmas Eve, the girls and I went over to Mom's house. I spent my time there lying in bed. My younger sister came into the room where I was, and mentioned that there was a known Christian preacher on TV, live from Toronto. I transferred to the sofa in the living room, and listened to the preacher talk about Jesus with such passion and love. Then he announced that they were going to have communion, encouraging everyone—including those watching by television—to participate. He gave the viewers time to get ready while explaining what communion meant: *"Communion means remembering and celebrating the crucifixion and resurrection of Jesus, which is redemption, salvation, and freedom from all the power of Satan that plagues our physical, emotional, and spiritual lives. Jesus on the cross destroyed the works of the devil in our lives so that we could be free!"*

"Jesus took bread, and when He had given thanks, He broke it and gave it to them, saying, 'This is My body, which is given for you. Do this in remembrance of me.'

And, likewise, Jesus said, 'This cup that is poured out for you is the new covenant in My blood.'"

(Luke 22:19-20).

Upon hearing of Jesus's ultimate *sacrifice of love* on the cross, for *all humanity*, my spirit was filled with hope, and an urgent need came upon me to participate in the communion in honor of Him for *His amazing act of love, for me and for the whole world!*

I asked Mom to bring some juice and bread enough for all of us to partake. Confused, she grabbed the juice jug and some bread, and brought it all to the coffee table.

As a family—Mom, Dad, my younger sister, her family, and my girls, my precious beautiful girls, Daisy and Cristal—we all gathered in the living room. We held our juice cups high in one hand, and our pieces of bread in the other, and as the preacher began partaking, we did, as well.

The whole process may have seemed religious and even ritualistic to some, but God's presence in the room was indisputable, indescribable, thick, and tangible! God was with us!

Then, suddenly, the preacher began speaking right to me! He said,

"There is a young lady, you are lying on a sofa, and you have pain all over your body, and doctors don't really know what is wrong with you. Get ready to receive your healing—NOW!"

There was no doubt in my spirit that the preacher was talking to me, for at the same time, God's presence came over me, touching my body and removing all the fatigue and weakness that had plagued me for months. My physical body was filled with strength, and my heart with exuberant joy.

I got up from the sofa and began walking around the living room, rejoicing and sharing the miracle I had just received from Jesus with my family.

"He touched me! He touched me!" I exclaimed.

My family listened and watched me, speechless.

My girls and I hugged each other tightly, tears of happiness, joy and hope running down our cheeks, at the wonderful miracle Jesus had just performed in *our* lives. While holding each other, I said to my girls,

"We can go home now, and be a family, a happy family, because Jesus is with us, and He will take care of us. We will find a church, and go and worship Him, together!"

My journey for happiness was over. I had finally found what I had been looking and longing for all of my life in Jesus!

The weeks and months rolled by, and I had been given the strength I needed to care for my girls. My body still ached strangely, and the ice-cold sweats in my legs still lingered some, but I was learning from reading

God's promises, which is His word, that what God begins, He finishes!

> *"Being confident of this, that He (God) who began a good work in you will carry it on to completion."*
> —*Philippians 1:6*

Faithless Prayer from the Unexpected

My girls and I visited our first church. Having read God's promise in the book of James 5:14, I asked the senior pastor if he would pray for me and anoint me with oil, quoting to him the promise in James 5,

"Is any sick among you? Let him call for the elders of the church; and let them pray over him, anointing him with oil in the name of the Lord. And the prayer of faith shall save the sick, and the Lord shall raise him up; and if he has committed any sins, they shall be forgiven him."

But the preacher's answer confused and unsettled me.

"I am sorry," he said. "I cannot pray for you to be healed because I don't know God's will for you in this matter."

I couldn't believe what I was hearing, especially coming from a pastor.

I said, "Pastor, God's *will* is to heal *all* who ask and believe! It says so in his word in Mark 11:24. It's one of His promises! God will not go back on His Word!"

But the pastor stubbornly argued against it, and I settled for a weak, powerless prayer.

When I walked out of the church holding my girls' hands, I knew that this was *not* the church for us. I prayed to God while I drove away, asking that He would reveal himself to the pastor who was lacking urgent revelation of God's promises.

Years later, this same pastor died of an illness, declaring, "Whatever God's will for me, I will accept. If He wants to heal me, then so be it. If not, then so be it."

It was clear that this pastor's confession, was not one of faith when it came to healing.

"*He—Jesus—was wounded for our transgressions, bruised for our iniquities. The punishment that brought us peace was upon Him. And by His stripes, we are healed.*" —Isaiah 53:5

After visiting a few churches, we settled on one, and attended faithfully for many years.

Breaking Curses

At home, I spent much of my time seeking God, and the more I did, the more the Lord revealed Himself to me. He began showing me curses that were in my family that had attached themselves to me, even from generations past. As He did, He told me that, just as I had rebuked and ordered Satan to let go of my soul in Jesus's name when he was ready to take me to hell, I must do the same against these curses. I was to rebuke them in Jesus's name. So I did, and in the process, began forgiving and releasing individuals who had wounded me throughout the years. And I felt myself becoming free within.

Andrea Edwards

Brick Walls

Around the same time, I went shopping at a familiar place where a certain cashier had always been rude to me, and I was rude right back. However, things were different now.

I was a Christian, and I was going to love her and tell her about Jesus. I went to cash out, and there she was, rude as ever, if not worse. Well, my Christianity went right out the window, and I fired back with attitude.

On my way out, I was fuming, talking to God and justifying my actions toward her, trying to convince God that, after all, not *everyone* is heaven bound.

Well, talk about conviction hitting me like a ton of bricks! I couldn't believe what had just come out of my mouth, from a girl who had been so close to hell herself!

I wondered, how, now that I was a Christian, I could still behave this way.

Why hadn't I turned the other cheek? Why did I have to repay evil for evil? I should have shared the love of Jesus with her; but instead, I had told her off and wished her to hell!

When I arrived home, I went straight to my room and sat on the edge of my bed, crying out to God with sorrow and repentance in my heart. I said,

"Jesus, I am so sorry! Please forgive me! But answer me, Lord. If I am now a Christian, why do I behave like this? Why haven't You delivered me from this bad attitude? Please help me! Please set me free! I want to tell people about You, Lord, and I want to truly love them like You love them, bad attitude and all. Please help me, Jesus!

Help me change!"

Suddenly, I was in a vision, and I heard the voice of the Lord saying,

"Andrea, I love you! Come out!"

I could see a picture of *me* hiding behind brick walls inside of myself. The Lord was asking me to come out from the prison I was in. In the vision, I had an understanding that I had been imprisoned behind those brick walls for many years, to protect myself from the pains I had suffered at the hands of many. It was only normal for a wounded heart to retreat to a prison where it seemed safer, but a prison, nonetheless.

I responded, "I am afraid, Lord!"

The Lord asked, "Afraid of what?"

I answered, "Afraid that people won't like me. Afraid that people will hurt and reject me as they always have."

I began naming the many reasons why people didn't like me, as if trying to convince God that I was truly unlovable.

Then the Lord spoke to me again and said,

"Andrea, I love you! I love everything about you! I created you just the way you are. I formed you in your mother's womb. Before your mother knew you, I knew you. You, your personality, were My idea, and I love everything about you! I love you, Andrea! I love you, Andrea! I love you, Andrea! Don't be afraid. Come out."

I could see the Lord holding out His hands to me so that I would take a step forward, toward Him. With tears running down my face, I answered, "Here I am, Lord. Here I am."

And in the natural realm, I took a step away from my bed toward Him to show Him that I, Andrea, who had been in hiding for so long, was answering His call. I was coming out!

As soon as I took a physical step forward, I saw the walls that had kept me captive and imprisoned for so long come crashing down within me, and I saw myself walking right into the loving arms of Jesus! I began crying tears of joy, rejoicing at the freedom that I was experiencing! Once again, God had come to my rescue with yet another amazing miracle! I was not hiding in fear any longer. Andrea was free indeed!

Jesus says, "For whom the Son sets free, is free indeed!"—John 8:36

As the years passed, I came across the familiar cashier often, and felt nothing but compassion for her. And years later, I had the opportunity to share God's love with her.

Healed

I knew and felt that I had reached a point in my spiritual life where I had become grounded in God, for I had tasted the goodness of the Lord enough to know that there was no comparison out in the secular world. I had also tapped into the authority found in Jesus's name, and was using it to destroy the plans of the devil in my life, and of those people the Lord would show me while in prayer.

God was working in my girls' hearts, as well. Their faces radiated the peace and bliss that could only come from God. We were truly a happy family!

The summer of 1995 arrived and, on a warm, sunny Sunday morning while my girls and I were driving to church, singing along to worship songs, I noticed that the pain in my body had suddenly vanished. Just like that, I was healed! With tears streaming down my face, I thanked the Lord for yet another expected miracle. God was a promise keeper, true to His word!

Roger, whom I had nicknamed "the Faithful," continued calling me in the hope that we would resume our relationship. But there was no turning back for this girl. I was truly happy and completely satisfied with my new life. Nevertheless, Roger was in love with me, and he wouldn't give up.

One day, he accompanied me to a water spring and, while we drove with my worship music playing in the background, I felt God's tangible presence and so began worshiping the Lord out loud. After a few minutes, Roger said, "Andrea, when you speak about God, and sing His songs, you make Him sound so real. I'd like to know Him that way, too."

Surprised at his words, I wondered if perhaps the Lord was calling Roger, too.

As you can see, I still had much growing up in the Lord to do.

*The gift of salvation is God's gift to **ALL**! His desire is for **all** to be saved! And all who call upon Jesus's name shall be saved!*

Eventually, Roger surrendered his heart to Jesus, and the change that followed was genuine.

I began praying that God would bring Roger a good Christian wife who would help him with his Christian walk, and I decided to give God a helping hand in the process so that Roger would stop dreaming about being with me, something that could never be. My prayer for Roger was about to be answered—but not in the way I thought it would be.

Two Prophecies

While I was praying during a church service in 1996, a lady filled with the holy spirit came to prophesy over me. She said that the Lord had a husband for me. When I heard the prophecy, I was confused because, having been married and divorced once had me believing that I could never be married again. I had come to accept God's will for me—or what I thought was His will for me—in that matter, and I was truly satisfied with my life.

Nevertheless, when I got home, I sat on the edge of my bed as I usually did when I had questions roaming through my mind. I asked the Lord if this was indeed a word from Him, to confirm it. And as I searched the scriptures, He did.

My husband had been unfaithful to me. According to the bible, that meant that I was free to marry (with a believer), if I so desired. I had God's permission to marry, if He chose to bless me with a husband.

Nonetheless, the Lord and my girls had my undivided attention. If God indeed had a husband for me, I wasn't going to go looking for one. God would have to bring him to me.

Two months later, as I stood praying during another church service, two ladies came over to me and began prophesying that God had a husband for me. When the words were spoken to me, they witnessed with my spirit, and I was filled with gratitude toward God that He would choose to bless me with a husband. The desire for a husband was given birth to at that very moment.

When I got home that night, I sat at the edge of my bed, feeling ever so thankful that God had a husband for me.

I said,

"My Lord, you have a husband for me! Thank you! When I fall asleep tonight, will You give me a dream of my husband, and show me what He looks like?"

As I fell asleep that night, I had a dream. And let me tell you, God has a sense of humor!

The "Husband Dream"

In my dream, I was holding a baby boy in my arms. Mom and I were both sitting on the same sofa and I was showing her the baby boy, saying, "Look, Mom, he is of my flesh! He is of my flesh!" And I kept repeating the same words: "He is of my flesh."

The little boy had brown hair and light skin.

Mom looked and said, "Yes, Andrea, he is of your flesh, but he is not your child, he is your husband!"

As I held the baby boy, I looked at him and realized that he *was* my husband, and suddenly the baby boy began to grow so fast before our eyes that we were amazed! Then I heard the voice of the Lord saying to me, "Andrea, this is your husband. He is only a baby in the spirit now, but he is growing fast."

I woke up the following morning with a great big smile, bubbling up with joy. Laughing out loud, I said,

"Oh my Lord, You have such a funny sense of humor!"

Confirmation

A few days passed and Roger called, as usual, to ask if I needed any help with anything. At that very moment, I had been trying to put curtains up, but was having trouble because the apartment windows were very high and the chair I was using didn't allow me to reach to the top. Roger came over to help me immediately.

Mom showed up while Roger was busy working on the curtains, and soon after he left, Mom was on her way out the door, too. Before she walked out, she turned around and said something that took me by surprise.

"Andrea," she said, "if God has a husband for you, as you say, I think it would be Roger."

I had shared the husband prophecies with Mom, mainly to get her reaction and prepare her so that when God's word came to pass she would accept it. But I hadn't shared the dream, and in the dream Mom had recognized my husband. Could she be confirming it now in the natural realm?

By her statement, she was also giving me her blessing to marry, which was important to me, and another miracle in itself.

Then all of a sudden, when Mom left, it hit me, and it hit me hard! "Oh God, Roger? Roger! Roger is going to be my husband?!"

I went to my room in somewhat of a panic, letting God know that even though I liked Roger and respected him as a man, I had lost my physical attraction to him since I had surrendered my life to Him. And I told God that if, indeed, Roger was the husband He had chosen for me, I needed to be physically attracted to him again, or I wasn't getting married!

Counterfeit

As the weeks rolled by, I met a Christian man, well-established in the ministry in a very large church. We met in a service, where he was preaching. We spoke briefly and parted ways. A few weeks passed and one day when I arrived at my church, I had a message from the secretary that a Mr. So-and-So was looking for me. He shared that he had been phoning all the churches in my town looking for a Spanish girl named Andrea. I was shocked, and thought, "Could this be the man God has for me?"

Before calling him, I shared the news with my pastor's wife, seeking guidance in the matter, and she thought that surely the odds were on my side. I returned his call and, and we went on a date.

He wasted no time and came right to the point, letting me know his intentions for our meeting. He said he was very attracted to me and told me that he was considering having me as his wife. He proceeded to tell me how things would be, step by step, if I accepted his offer. I knew immediately in my heart that this was *not* the man for me, so I gladly declined his offer.

Others also came my way, desiring me as their wife, but I knew they were not God's choice for me, but someone else's.

Andrea Edwards

Download from Heaven

Then one sunny day on my birthday, I was doing a load of laundry at Roger's house. I was busy in the laundry room, when Roger came in. While he stood there talking to me, all of a sudden, the Lord supernaturally downloaded love into my heart for Roger.

As I continued listening to Roger speak, there was no doubt in me that I loved this man, and that I wanted to take care of him in every way a godly, loving wife would care for her husband—even intimately!

Thinking that perhaps these feelings were being brought on by the devil, I waited nervously for my laundry to be done, and then rushed home.

One thing I had learned in my Christian walk was that I wasn't going to be led away from God by my fleshly desires.

When I got home, I went directly to my bedroom and sat on the edge of my bed asking God to set me free from the feelings that had suddenly come upon me.

I chose not to see Roger for a few weeks, as I waited for the Lord's guidance, but my every thought was consumed with him. Then one-night while in prayer, God spoke to me encouraging me that the love I felt for Roger was indeed from Him. God had chosen to supernaturally download it into my heart on my birthday. Another miracle from my heavenly Papa!

Roger and I were soon married, and we have spent many fabulous, fun, and amazing years together!

We contemplate often and are amazed at what God has done in us, and continues to do, daily!

Jesus is truly the foundation and center of our lives, therefore our marriage.

When you invite God to be the center of your life, He will make your dreams come true!

Chapter Twelve

Forgiveness

While driving up north one day in 1996, I had a supernatural vision. I suddenly saw two hearts appear in the sky that had my mother's and father's faces inside of them. The hearts, which were three-dimensional, began to come closer to me. I could clearly see that these hearts were broken in many pieces, and had been since childhood. Then I heard the voice of the Lord say to me,

"Andrea, do you see their hearts?"

I said, "Yes, Lord. I see them."

He said, "Their hearts are broken from a life of pain. I want to heal their hearts, just like I have healed yours."

Feeling the Lord's love and compassion for my parents, I responded,

"Yes, Lord. Yes!"

Upon responding, I began to weep with sobs, groans, and tears that came from the very pit of my stomach, and I knew that it was the Holy Spirit interceding for my parents to be healed—through me.

After the vision, I had a clear understanding of my parents' hearts, and forgiveness and love towards them came into my heart like a refreshing river, to stay.

The power of forgiveness flows through a surrendered heart.

In my family's lives, God is orchestrating a beautiful masterpiece. Throughout the years, God has shown me tangible evidence of His amazing work in their lives, blessing my heart greatly.

"Being confident of this, that He who began a good work in you will carry it on to completion until the day of Christ Jesus."
—*Philippians 1:6*

When I look back and contemplate my life, I see Gods hand of love and protection over me.

My life could have been worse. I could have simply gone on existing loaded up with pain. Or worse yet, I could have died without crying out to Jesus, that would of been an eternal catastrophe.

The storms and valleys, the darkness, the pains have brought me to Jesus.

I have learned to trust Him with my life.

I don't look back with regret. I look back and I clearly see that since the day I was conceived, my Heavenly Father has Loved me!

I have been the recipient of God's amazing love. His love, forgiveness and acceptance of me has flowed deeply into my whole being and healed my broken heart. Unmeasurable love, the kind that cannot be explained, for it is too deep for words. Its vast and greatness one can never truly fathom. Its power has captivated me. God's love I have embraced, fully!

Because of His amazing love, I have also forgiven *everyone* who has ever hurt me, including those mentioned in this book.

I will never cease to drink from the river of forgiveness. Even now I feel it flowing through me, so freeing upon my soul!

Forgiveness is not a choice
It's a must, to be free,
and enter heaven!

God says to you:

*"If you put your trust in Me,
whatever your darkness may be,
it will not overtake you.
For I Jesus, I am the Light of the world.
If you ask Me into your heart,
I will rescue you out of the darkness,
into My glorious Light!
For Nothing is Impossible for Me!"*

"I am the Light of the world; he who follows Me will not walk in the darkness, but will have the Light of life." John 8:12

Jesus.

"Andrea, write down the things I have done in your life, because I want My people to know, THAT ALL THINGS ARE POSSIBLE WITH ME! Publish My glorious deeds among the nations.
Tell everyone about the amazing things I do."
-1 Chronicles 16:24
God (2005)

"Yes, Lord!"
Andrea Edwards (2005)

"Mission completed!"
Andrea Edwards (2015)

Prayer of Salvation:

Do you want Jesus in your heart? Repeat this prayer, and Jesus will come and make his home in your heart:

"Dear Jesus, please forgive me for all my sins. Wash me and cleanse me with Your precious blood that You shed on the cross for me to cleanse me from all sin. Become my Lord and my Savior at this very moment. In Jesus's name, I pray. Amen."

"For God so loved the world that he gave His one and only Son, that whoever believes in Him shall not perish but have eternal life. For God did not send His Son into the world to condemn the world, but to save the world through Him. For God did not send His Son into the world to condemn the world, but to SAVE the world through Him"

John 3:16-17

About the Author

Andrea Edwards received a Lay-Pastoral counseling certificate in 1997-1998, and began volunteering in a local Jail, and in Hospitals, sharing the love of God. She is also involved with different outreaches in her community.

She is in the process of writing and publishing other books: from Devotionals, Short Stories, Children, youth and young adult books.

For more information on Andrea Edwards,

And to invite her as a Speaker, you may contact her through email or website.

www.rescuedbythelight.com

Printed in Canada